Posttraumatic Stress Disorder in Litigation

Guidelines for Forensic Assessment

Posttraumatic Stress Disorder in Litigation

Guidelines for Forensic Assessment

Edited by
Robert I. Simon, M.D.

Clinical Professor of Psychiatry
Director, Program in Psychiatry and Law
Georgetown University School of Medicine
Washington, D.C.

Washington, DC
London, England

Copyright © 1995 American Psychiatric Press, Inc.
ALL RIGHTS RESERVED
Manufactured in the United States of America on acid-free paper
98 97 96 95   4 3 2 1
First Edition

American Psychiatric Press, Inc.
1400 K Street, N.W., Washington, DC   20005

Library of Congress Cataloging-in-Publication Data
Posttraumatic stress disorder in litigation : guidelines for forensic
   assessment / edited by Robert I. Simon. — 1st ed.
        p.   cm.
   Includes bibliographical references and index.
   ISBN 0-88048-687-2 (casebound : alk. paper)
   1. Post-traumatic stress disorder—Diagnosis.   2. Post-traumatic
stress disorder—Law and legislation.   I. Simon, Robert I.
   [DNLM: 1. Stress Disorders, Post-Traumatic—psychology—United
States.   2. Forensic Psychiatry—United States—legislation.   WM 33
AA1 P75   1995]
RA1152.P67P67   1995
614'.1—dc20
DNLM/DLC
for Library of Congress   94-30643
                                                                          CIP

British Library Cataloguing in Publication Data
A CIP record is available from the British Library.

This book is dedicated to assisting all parties
in psychic injury litigation by the provision of
sound clinical guidelines for forensic assessment.

**Yet man is born unto trouble,
as the sparks fly upward.**

—Job 5:7

Contents

Contributors xi

Foreword xiii
    Richard L. Goldberg, M.D.

Preface xv
    Robert I. Simon, M.D.

Acknowledgments xvii

Introduction xix
    Ralph Slovenko, L.L.B., Ph.D.

1   Persistent Reexperiences in Psychiatry and Law: Current and
    Future Trends in Posttraumatic Stress Disorder Litigation   1
    Daniel W. Shuman, J.D.

2   Recent Research Findings on the Diagnosis of Posttraumatic
    Stress Disorder: Prevalence, Course, Comorbidity, and Risk . . . 13
    Bonnie L. Green, Ph.D.

3   Toward the Development of Guidelines in the Forensic
    Psychiatric Examination of Posttraumatic Stress Disorder
    Claimants 31
    Robert I. Simon, M.D.

4   Guidelines for the Psychiatric Examination of Posttraumatic
    Stress Disorder in Children and Adolescents 85
    Kathleen M. Quinn, M.D.

5   Guidelines for the Forensic Psychological Assessment of
Posttraumatic Stress Disorder Claimants 99
Terence M. Keane, Ph.D.

6   Guidelines for the Evaluation of Malingering in
Posttraumatic Stress Disorder 117
Phillip J. Resnick, M.D.

Index 135

Contributors

Richard L. Goldberg, M.D.
Professor and Chairman, Department of Psychiatry,
Georgetown University School of Medicine, Washington, D.C.

Bonnie L. Green, Ph.D.
Professor of Psychiatry, Department of Psychiatry,
Georgetown University School of Medicine, Washington, D.C.

Terence M. Keane, Ph.D.
Director, National Center for PTSD—Boston,
Department of Veterans Affairs Medical Center,
Boston, Massachusetts; Chief, Division of Medical Psychology,
Tufts University School of Medicine, Boston, Massachusetts

Kathleen M. Quinn, M.D.
Associate Clinical Professor of Psychiatry, Case Western University
School of Medicine; Director of Forensic Psychiatry,
Cleveland Clinic Foundation, Cleveland, Ohio

Phillip J. Resnick, M.D.
Professor of Psychiatry, Director of Forensic Psychiatry,
Case Western University School of Medicine, Cleveland, Ohio

Daniel W. Shuman, J.D.
Professor of Law, Southern Methodist University School of Law,
Dallas, Texas

Robert I. Simon, M.D.
Clinical Professor of Psychiatry and Director, Program in Psychiatry and
Law, Department of Psychiatry, Georgetown University
School of Medicine, Washington, D.C.

Ralph Slovenko, L.L.B., Ph.D.
Professor of Law and Psychiatry, Wayne State University Law School,
Detroit, Michigan

Foreword

Hundreds of millions of dollars are paid each year to psychological injury claimants for injuries that include complaints of posttraumatic stress disorder (PTSD). In many instances, there are no guidelines for proper assessment of the psychological and psychiatric data involved in these claims. Thus some seriously injured individuals are undercompensated, whereas others, who have no proximate relationship between their symptoms and behaviors and the legal cause of action, are improperly compensated.

There are several problem areas in the forensic assessment of PTSD litigants. PTSD often occurs comorbidly with other psychiatric disorders, making differentiation very difficult. Preexisting traits and states may contribute to shaping PTSD. Individuals demonstrate various vulnerabilities for developing the full spectrum of signs and symptoms of this disorder. PTSD is a disorder that can be malingered. The phenomenon of PTSD and the course of illness may be very different in unique populations of individuals such as children. And, finally, the severity of disability resulting from PTSD can be difficult to quantify.

Robert I. Simon, M.D., director of Georgetown University's Program in Psychiatry and Law, has organized the PTSD in Litigation Project and obtained original articles from national experts for this book, *Posttraumatic Stress Disorder in Litigation: Guidelines for Forensic Assessment.* This work addresses a diverse audience of individuals with an interest in forensic psychiatry by shedding light on important issues relating to PTSD litigation. What has emerged are guidelines for forensic assessment that can serve both plaintiffs and defendants in litigation involving PTSD claims. I have no doubt that this book will serve as essential and comprehensive reading for all those interested in forensic psychiatry and, particularly, the growing field of psychological injury litigation.

Richard L. Goldberg, M.D.
Professor and Chairman
Department of Psychiatry
Georgetown University School of Medicine

Preface

When the diagnosis of posttraumatic stress disorder (PTSD) was first officially created by DSM-III in 1980, I do not think that anyone fully appreciated the impact it would have on psychic injury litigation. Since then, with the burgeoning of litigation, PTSD has become a growth industry. No diagnosis in American psychiatry has had such a profound influence on civil and criminal law. PTSD has been alleged in a wide variety of claims. Just a few examples include malpractice, personal injury, sexual harassment, child abuse, and as an insanity defense in criminal cases. Some commentators have dubbed PTSD the "black hole" of litigation, perhaps an exasperated exaggeration.

PTSD lends itself well to litigation. It is, by definition, incident specific, thus creating the impression that multiple causation seen in most other psychiatric disorders does not exist when PTSD is alleged. The allegations that a claimant is suffering from PTSD are relatively easy to assert but difficult to defend because the symptoms are subjective, except for behavioral reenactments of the trauma.

Guidelines for the forensic psychiatric and psychological assessment of PTSD claimants do not exist. In litigation, it is quite common to find the diagnosis of PTSD made without any attempt to follow the diagnostic criteria for this disorder. Moreover, the forensic examiner may rely totally on the subjective reporting of the claimant, failing to consult other sources of information. Cases are encountered in which the life of the claimant appears to begin with the litigation. In other words, no past history is obtained. In assessing impairment and disability, one also encounters forensic examiners relying on personal impressions rather than established assessment methods.

It is vitally important for all the legal parties involved that forensic examiners perform credible psychiatric or psychological examinations of PTSD claimants. The guidelines for evaluation of PTSD claimants proposed in this book are dedicated to that end. Favoring neither the plaintiff nor the defendant, this book represents an initial effort to bring some direction and discipline to this complex area of psychic injury litigation. It is hoped that this book will spark a continuing dialogue among mental health professionals, the legal community, and third-party payers concerning improvement of psychiatric and psychological assessment of PTSD claimants.

Both plaintiffs and defendants should benefit from this book's guidelines. A credible forensic evaluation obviously strengthens a plaintiff's genuine PTSD claim. When a credible evaluation is performed, the defendant is also in a better position to fairly compensate a truly injured individual while defending vigorously against the spurious claim.

Robert I. Simon. M.D.

Acknowledgments

The Program in Psychiatry and Law at Georgetown University School of Medicine owes its existence to the unwavering support and encouragement of Richard L. Goldberg, M.D., Professor and Chairman of the Department of Psychiatry. His foresight and leadership in helping launch the successful PTSD in Litigation Project led to the creation and publication of this book.

This work is made possible by the scholarly contributions of my colleagues who are nationally recognized experts in the legal, research, or forensic psychiatric aspects of PTSD. The quality and the singular importance of their individual chapters on PTSD in litigation will stand alone for some time to come. I hope those who find this book useful will feel some of the gratitude I now express in full measure for their excellent contributions.

Special appreciation goes to Peter B. Silvain, Ph.D., Clinical Associate Professor of Psychiatry and Pamela H. Silvain, Ph.D., Clinical Assistant Professor of Psychiatry. Both served as valued faculty advisors to the project.

I want to express my personal gratitude to Carol C. Nadelson, M.D., Editor-in-Chief, and Claire Reinburg, Editorial Director, American Psychiatric Press, for their early recognition of the broad relevance of the topic of PTSD in litigation and their enthusiastic support for publishing this book.

Introduction

In 1992, the Program in Psychiatry and Law at Georgetown University, under the leadership of Dr. Robert I. Simon, sponsored a standards development conference on the forensic assessment of claimants of posttraumatic stress disorder (PTSD). The articles presented at the conference have undergone revision and appear in this book, along with an additional chapter on guidelines for psychological testing of PTSD litigants.

Standards are important in diagnosis, for without them the same condition may be given different labels, with the result that the clinician may overlook syndromes known to respond to other treatments and may be misleading to insurers and the courts. A diagnostic category, with its defining elements, alerts the clinician to the possibility that a patient's condition is unlike disorders subsumed under other categories. Questions have arisen, however, as to the validity of defining the cluster of symptoms following trauma as a distinct and unique entity. Stress or trauma has been generally presumed to increase the risk of all pathology, physical and mental. Multiple personality, for example, is said to be the result of child abuse.

In Chapter 2 of this volume, Dr. Bonnie L. Green discusses new research and its implications for the diagnosis of PTSD. Dr. Green notes the increasing evidence that exposure to multiple events is more common than previously thought and that multiple exposure increases the risk for the development of PTSD following the target event. In Chapter 3, Dr. Simon elaborates on the development of guidelines for the forensic psychiatric examination of the PTSD claimant. He discusses the diagnostic criteria for PTSD and notes that with litigation burgeoning, PTSD has become a growth industry.

The American Psychiatric Association's first Diagnostic and Statistical Manual, published in 1952, listed stress response syndromes under the heading of "gross stress reactions." In DSM-II, published in 1968, however, trauma-related disorders were conceptualized as just one example of situational disorders. The term *traumatic neurosis*, though not an official classification, gained currency, especially among forensic psychiatrists. Mainly at the persistence of forensic psychiatrists, DSM-III, published in 1980, listed PTSD. As the term *neurosis* is generally abandoned in DSM-III, it settled on PTSD as a subcategory under anxiety disorders.

For the classification in DSM-III, there was intense controversy over whether PTSD was an anxiety or a dissociative disorder. For DSM-IV, published in 1994, the Advisory Subcommittee on PTSD was reportedly unanimous in classifying PTSD as a new stress response category.

PTSD is the most recent of the many names, most of them in the common vernacular, that have been used to describe the mental suffering of victims of trauma. These terms include the following: *neurosis following trauma, neurosis following accident, terror neurosis (schreckneurose), acute neurotic reaction, triggered neurosis, postaccident anxiety syndrome, posttraumatic hysteria, hysterical paralysis, social neurosis, personal injury neurosis, industrial neurosis, accident neurosis, occupational neurosis, litigation neurosis, justice neurosis, compensation neurosis, compensationitis, desire neurosis, unconscious malingering, retirement neurosis, pension neurosis, fate neurosis,* and *secondary gain neurosis.*

Under DSM-III, the cluster of symptoms that constituted PTSD included a distinctively etiological element, namely, a stressor of an extraordinary magnitude. For a diagnosis of PTSD, the DSM specifies a stressor that is "outside the range of usual human experience" and that would be "markedly distressing to almost anyone." The manual gives examples of "common experiences" that do not qualify for PTSD—"simple bereavement, chronic illness, business losses, or marital conflict" (American Psychiatric Association 1980, p. 247). The other criteria set out in the manual for a diagnosis of PTSD are a reexperiencing of the trauma in flashbacks or recollections, numbing of responsiveness, and any two symptoms from a list of predominantly anxious and depressive symptoms.

The criterion of an extreme stressor and reexperiencing of the trauma does not explicitly appear in the definition of any other diagnosis in DSM. A number of researchers have found patients who meet symptom criteria for PTSD without meeting the stressor criterion. Dr. Green, who served on the advisory committee for the PTSD diagnosis for DSM-III-R and on the DSM-IV PTSD advisory committee, reports that the most debate regarding this diagnosis has centered on the definition of the stressor criterion and also on whether there should be additional diagnosis that reflect responses to traumatic events. DSM-IV omits the phrase "outside the range of usual human experience," but like DSM-III-R it requires "an event or events that involved actual or threatened death or serious injury, or a threat to the physical integrity of self or others" (American Psychiatric Association 1994, p. 427). It retains the three categories of symptoms—an intrusive and vivid recall of the trauma, a numbing of feelings and a psychic dissociation from reality, and increased arousal, or hypersensitive nerves.

On the basis of the duration of symptoms, DSM distinguishes two subtypes of PTSD: symptoms that begin immediately or soon after the trauma, and symptoms that begin at least 6 months after the trauma. The classification is based on evidence of acute, delayed, and intermittent or recurrent forms of PTSD.

The Veterans Administration, following its authorization in 1980 of compensation and other benefits for PTSD, delayed type, has received an increasingly large number of claims—mainly from Vietnam War veterans—for this disorder. Many ex-military individuals who are without insurance coverage have turned to the VA, alleging PTSD. Claimants present themselves to examiners, fully aware of the checklist of the diagnostic features of the disorder. In this situation, PTSD is often called a political diagnosis.

In criminal or civil cases, individuals may be highly motivated to malinger PTSD. Lawyers call them "designer" cases; forensic experts are ready to testify to PTSD. After all, who doesn't suffer trauma? In civil cases, of course, the primary motivation to malinger is financial gain. In the criminal justice system, a PTSD diagnosis may serve as a basis for an insanity defense, a reduction of charges, or mitigation of penalty. In particular, PTSD has been frequently claimed by Vietnam War veterans charged with crime. In the days of the Soviet Union, individuals charged with crime were asked whether they served in the Great Patriotic War; it was not necessary to medicalize an excuse.

In Chapter 6, Dr. Phillip J. Resnick sets out standards for the evaluation of malingering in PTSD. He concedes that the assessment of malingered psychiatric symptoms after traumatic events is difficult because reports of subjective symptoms are hard to verify. He provides indicators of genuine and malingered PTSD. Of course, evidence of an extraordinary stressor gives credibility to the claim of PTSD. In Chapter 4, Dr. Kathleen M. Quinn provides guidelines for the examination of PTSD in children. Although there is an extensive body of literature describing PTSD among adults, fewer studies of PTSD in children have been done.

Over the years the law has been concerned about the potential flood of litigation if compensation were awarded in cases of negligence that result in mental distress without accompanying physical impact or injury. On the other hand, for intentional wrongdoing, as in cases of assault, defamation, false imprisonment, invasion of privacy, and malicious prosecution, the law provided a remedy for mental distress. As a New York court said in 1896 in *Mitchell v. Rochester Railway Co.*,

If the right of recovery [for mental distress in negligence cases without physical impact or injury] should be once established, it would naturally result in a flood of litigation in cases where the injury complained of may be easily feigned without detection, and where the damages must rest upon mere conjecture or speculation. The difficulty which often exists in cases of alleged physical injury, in determining whether they exist, and if so, whether they were caused by the negligent act of the defendant, would not only be greatly increased, but a wide field would be opened for fictitious or speculative claims. To establish such a doctrine would be contrary to principles of public policy.

Since the mid-twentieth century, an increasing number of states, one by one, have removed the physical impact or injury limitation in negligence actions. The law in these states has moved from that of requiring physical impact or injury to allowing claims without insisting either that the victim feared for his or her own safety or that he or she even suffered physical injury such as a heart attack or miscarriage. Claims are now allowed for mental distress arising from seeing a relative or other person injured or endangered.

In all torts in which there is physical injury, damages are awarded for pain and suffering. In product liability cases, pain and suffering accounts for 50% of all damages. The awards are often absurdly high or pitifully low. Usually, juries simply award a plaintiff a multiple of the claimed medical expenses. As medical bills have mushroomed, so have pay-outs for pain and suffering. Large medical bills thus make out a strong case. Inflationary medical bills are to the advantage of a claimant (and the lawyer). Some reformers argue that pain and suffering awards should be abolished (or capped) and that only judgments based on economic loss should be allowed. In law, the term *damage* is used to describe the harm, and *damages* or *recovery* to indicate the award.

Wholly aside from the question of how far the law should go in protecting against emotional disturbance, there are difficult evidentiary questions of 1) fault, 2) causation, and 3) assessment of damages. The vulnerability of the victim is considered differently in each of these various elements that together constitute a tort.

For fault, the risk reasonably to be perceived determines the duty of care. Foreseeability is the traditional test. Thus a greater duty of care is imposed on a motorist when he or she sees a handicapped person or child crossing the street. When the vulnerability of a persor is not reasonably apparent, he or she may fairly be assumed to be an ordinary individual.

Negligence is failing to observe the care of a reasonable person in like circumstances. Instead of the standard of the reasonable person, the standard may be prescribed in a statute, as, for example, safety legislation.

For tort liability, not only must there be damage (injury), but it also must have been caused by the defendant's fault. In causation, the law looks for proximate cause. There is no litmus test for determining proximity, and there may be more than one proximate cause. Some courts use a foreseeability test, but usually the test is the *natural and probable* cause-and-effect relationship.

In every case, the question arises as to what extent a wrongdoer should have to answer for the consequences that his or her conduct has helped to produce. Some limitation must be placed on responsibility because the consequences of an act theoretically reach into infinity. A tugboat that hits a bridge may cause houses miles away to vibrate and collapse. Is there responsibility? Is the damage too remote? The connection between the wrongdoing and the harm done must be reasonable, the courts say.

Also, in assessing causation, there is the well-known expression, "The tortfeasor must take his victim as he finds him," so that peculiar vulnerability to harm does not excuse. However, it may be argued, sometimes successfully, that "the straw that broke the camel's back" is not a proximate cause.

The so-called delayed PTSD may be the result of a cumulation of events resulting in a crisis. (In law, the time period in the statute of limitations begins when the injury is "made known.") The proximate cause may arguably be either the earlier or a later event. The term *proximate* has connotations of nearness in time, but that is not its meaning in law. *Legal cause* or *responsible cause* are more appropriate terms, but those terms also leave much room for vagaries in decision making. In an increasing number of cases, the courts are saying that the determination of proximate cause is the province of judges not juries.

PTSD is a favored diagnosis by plaintiffs because it is incident specific. It tends to rule out other factors important to the determination of causation. Thus a plaintiff can argue that all of his or her psychological problems issue from the alleged traumatic event and not from myriad other sources encountered in life. A diagnosis of depression, on the other hand, opens the issue of causation to many factors other than the stated cause of action.

In days gone by, when the term *traumatic neurosis* was used, psychiatrists distinguished between a *true traumatic neurosis,* in which a healthy individual suffers emotional distress as a result of an overwhelming stress, and a *triggered neurosis,* in which a vulnerable individual decompensates as a result of stress that would be quite inconsequential to a healthy individual. Theoret-

Posttraumatic Stress Disorder in Litigation

ically, in law, however, the distinction is one without a difference, but, in the case of a triggered neurosis, the argument is made that the proximate cause is not a triggering event.

To be sure, trauma is a relative concept—stimulus in relation to the coping ability of an individual—yet when a stressor is not outside the range of common experience, the evidence tends to support a finding that it is not the proximate cause. Also when a stressor is not outside the range of common experience, it arouses suspicions of malingering, or it raises the issue of individual susceptibility and psychiatric comorbidity.

Widespread job instability has led to mounting disability claims. At the same time, it has led to a tightening of the concept of causation in workers' compensation. The Michigan Court of Appeals in 1991 ruled that mental disabilities are compensable only if "contributed to or aggravated or accelerated by the employment in a significant manner" and they arise "out of actual events of employment, not unfounded perceptions thereof" (*Sobh v. Frederick & Herrud* 1991).

In the determination of causation under workers' compensation, the Oregon Supreme Court observed the following:

> It seems that no problem in recent years has given courts and commissioners administering workers' compensation more difficulty than on-the-job mental stress which results in either emotional or physical illness. The causal relationship between employment stress and a resulting mental or emotional disorder presents one of the most complex issues in workers' compensation law. (*McGarrah v. SAIF* 1983, p. 161)

Teachers in public schools feel as though they are in combat. School teachers in Detroit (and elsewhere) say, "Why all the fuss about the PTSD of Vietnam War veterans? What about us?" In denying a teacher's claim, the Michigan Court of Appeals concluded the following:

> Workers' compensation benefits are not available just because a plaintiff established the existence of some incident or "event" which is upsetting to the plaintiff. There must be an injury. The Legislature has required the injury to be based upon "actual events" of employment. . . . This requirement would become meaningless if the ordinary, daily conditions of minutiae of employment were sufficient to support a mental disability claim. Thus, ordinary stresses of employment (existing in probably all jobs) are not sufficient to establish the required injury. . . . [The] plaintiff's allegations involved general stressful conditions that are common to all teachers. (*Boyle v. Detroit Board of Education* 1992, p. 260)

In assessing damages, testimony of the condition of the claimant before and after the occurrence of the stressor is crucial to the case. (Punitive damages are another matter.) The forensic examiners are called on to make a long-term assessment of impairment. The before-and-after testimony dwells on differences in personality, character traits, and behavior, such as outgoing vs. withdrawn, loving vs. indifferent, mild-mannered vs. abusive, reliable vs. erratic, and clean vs. slovenly. When preexisting psychological problems are aggravated, accelerated, or reactivated by trauma, a court may have qualms about ascribing the full injury to the defendant. As a matter of law, a jury is to discount what would have happened anyhow.

Law professors like to discuss the case of *Steinhauser v. Hertz Corp.* (1970). The case was settled upon remand to the trial court for proper jury instruction. In this case, the plaintiff, a 14-year-old girl, was a passenger in a car that was sideswiped. She and the other occupants in the car suffered no bodily injury, but within a few minutes after the accident, she began to behave in an unusual way. Her parents observed her to be "glassy-eyed," "upset," "highly agitated," "nervous," and "disturbed." In the following days things became steadily worse. She thought that she was being attacked and that knives, guns, and bullets were coming through the windows. She was hostile toward her parents and assaulted them. Becoming depressed, she attempted suicide. After observation and treatment in several hospitals, she was given a diagnosis of schizophrenic reaction, acute undifferentiated. In later treatment, she was given the diagnosis of chronic schizophrenic reaction.

Testimony at the trial was that the accident was "the precipitating cause" of her serious mental illness. According to the testimony, she had a "prepsychotic" personality prior to the accident but might nonetheless have been able to lead a normal life. The accident was "that last straw that breaks the camel's back," said one of the experts.

As the recital makes evident, two issues were before the jury: 1) the existence of a causal relationship between a rather slight accident and the plaintiff's undoubtedly serious illness, and 2) the assessment of harm. On the assessment of harm, the United States Second Circuit Court of Appeals specified what the jury should consider:

Although the fact that [the plaintiff] had latent psychotic tendencies would not defeat recovery if the accident was a precipitating cause of schizophrenia, this may have a significant bearing on the amount of damages. The defendants are entitled to explore the probability that the [plaintiff] might have developed schizophrenia in any event. While the evidence does not demonstrate that [the plaintiff] already had the disease, it does suggest that she was a good prospect. . . . [We have said] that if a defendant "succeeds in the establishing that the plaintiff's preexisting condition was bound to worsen . . . an appropriate discount should be made for the damages that would have been suffered even in the absence of the defendant's negligence.". . . It is no answer that exact prediction of [the plaintiff's] future apart from the accident is difficult or even impossible. However taxing such a problem may be for men who have devoted their lives to psychiatry, it is one for which a jury is ideally suited. (*Steinhauser v. Hertz Corp.* 1970, pp. 1173–1174)

Whatever the accuracy of the diagnosis, be it schizophrenia or PTSD, the question is what difference does a diagnosis make when before-and-after determines the measure of damage? A diagnosis is not necessary to establish what the claimant was able to do before and after the trauma. Lay witnesses can attest to that. Yet the DSM is state of the art and the forensic expert is invariably asked to label the claimant's suffering.

Theoretically, a diagnosis informs about prognosis. In general, claimants have an obligation to minimize their damages. In some cases, PTSD symptoms diminish over time, in association with many differing factors, whereas in other cases they do not diminish and in fact may worsen in the absence of treatment. A wide variety of factors may affect the course of PTSD, including coping mechanisms, social support, type and duration of stress, family functioning, personality, other disorders, and so on.

Expert testimony is essential regarding the prognosis for alleviation of a claimant's symptoms. The expert is called on to describe the various treatment alternatives and give indications of their likely results. A claimant has an obligation to minimize injury. Dr. Simon notes that a variety of effective psychological and psychopharmacologic treatments are available for individuals who have PTSD.

There is divided opinion on the admissibility of syndrome evidence in criminal or civil cases to establish that a particular traumatic event or stressor actually occurred. Is the credibility of a victim claiming rape, for example, supported by evidence matching her trauma with the trauma pattern of other rape victims? Is a single posttraumatic stress syndrome the pathway of a stressor? Do all victims of a particular stressor react in the same manner? What is the relation between symptoms and stressor? The presence of PTSD symptoms presumes, by definition, an antecedent traumatic stressor, but, as Dr. Simon points out, arguing backward from the claimant's PTSD to specific causes or events as a defense in criminal cases, or as a basis for a claim for damages in tort cases, is problematic.

Various syndromes—rape trauma, battered spouse, child sexual abuse, and so forth—are not currently enumerated as separate syndromes or as subcategories of PTSD in the DSM, but forensic experts testify about them in court. Does a rape trauma syndrome, for example, accurately describe the behavior of women who have been sexually assaulted? Does that syndrome differ depending on the age, socioeconomic status, or other characteristics of the woman? Law Professor Daniel W. Shuman has argued that psychiatry has an obligation to assist the courts in accurately evaluating the various syndromes. Otherwise, he says, psychiatry may well suffer a loss of credibility and the judicial system a loss of accuracy (Shuman 1989).

These and other issues are richly discussed in this publication. This book will be of much interest to a multidisciplinary audience.

Ralph Slovenko, L.L.B., Ph.D.
Professor of Law and Psychiatry
Wayne State University Law School

References

American Psychiatric Association: Diagnostic and Statistical Manual: Mental Disorders. Washington, DC, American Psychiatric Association, 1952

American Psychiatric Association: Diagnostic and Statistical Manual of Mental Disorders, 2nd Edition. Washington, DC, American Psychiatric Association, 1968

American Psychiatric Association: Diagnostic and Statistical Manual of Mental Disorders, 3rd Edition. Washington, DC, American Psychiatric Association, 1980

American Psychiatric Association: Diagnostic and Statistical Manual of Mental Disorders, 3rd Edition, Revised. Washington, DC, American Psychiatric Association, 1987

American Psychiatric Association: Diagnostic and Statistical Manual of Mental Disorders, 4th Edition. Washington, DC, American Psychiatric Association, 1994

Boyle v Detroit Board of Education, 197 Mich App 255 (1992)

McGarrah v SAIF, 296 Or 145, 675 P2d 159 (1983)

Mitchell v Rochester Railway Co, 151 NY 107, 45 NE 354 (1896)

Shuman DW: The Diagnostic and Statistical Manual of Mental Disorders in the courts. Bull Am Acad Psychiatry Law 17:25–32, 1989

Sobh v Frederick & Herrud, 189 Mich App 24, 472 NW2d 8 (1991)

Steinhauser v Hertz Corp, 421 F2d 1169 (2d Cir 1970)

Chapter 1

Persistent Reexperiences in Psychiatry and Law

Current and Future Trends in Posttraumatic Stress Disorder Litigation

Daniel W. Shuman, J.D.

> *I am curiously weak, weak as if recovering from a long illness. I begin to feel it more in my head. I sleep well and eat well; but I write a half a dozen words and turn faint and sick.*

> —Charles Dickens' reaction to the crash of a train in which he was traveling that killed and injured numerous other passengers but left Dickens without physical injury (qtd. in Mendelson 1987, p. 48).

Two overarching considerations shape the trends in civil litigation seeking an award of damages for injuries diagnosed as a posttraumatic stress disorder (PTSD). One consideration is diagnostic nomenclature; what is a recognized psychiatric disorder? The other consideration is the law of damages; what is a compensable legal injury, and what evidence is admissible to support these claims?

As Mendelson (1987) has stated, "One of the enduring problems in the

I gratefully acknowledge a grant from the M. D. Anderson Foundation to support research for this work.

1

practice of forensic psychiatry is that of nomenclature" (p. 45). The concept encapsulated by PTSD is not new. What we now think of as PTSD has
been discussed in the psychiatric literature using different diagnostic nomenclature for at least 100 years (Modlin 1985). Why then is PTSD litigation only a recent phenomenon?

The diagnostic nomenclature of PTSD serves as a compelling example
of the power of language and its role in shaping the course of history
(White 1985). Consider some of the late-nineteenth-century and early-
twentieth-century diagnostic nomenclature addressing what would now be
regarded as PTSD, such as *railway spine* (Erichsen 1882) and *shell shock*
(Mott 1917). That diagnostic nomenclature was narrow in scope and did
not threaten to sweep much within its grasp. Only the self-contained uni-
verse of railroad passengers and combat veterans could fit within the diagnostic nomenclature. And the nomenclature implied a self-limiting
disorder as well as a degree of blameworthiness or preexisting weakness of
the victim that would likely limit the sympathy of a judge or jury. The early
language of psychiatry did not facilitate claims for what is now diagnosed
as PTSD.

The legal rules governing the receipt of evidence through the first half
of this century also served as a powerful limit on claims for what is now
diagnosed as PTSD. The rules of evidence were biased against the admissibility of expert testimony and in favor of lay witness testimony. The role of
the jury was to resolve cases based on a presentation by facts by lay witnesses
and to draw any inferences or reach any opinions necessary to the verdict
guided by its own insights whenever possible. Expert testimony was admissible only when the evidence was thought to be beyond the capacity of the
judge or jury to understand without expert assistance (Shuman 1986). Not
only were courts reluctant to admit expert testimony, but a high threshold
existed for a witness to qualify as an expert. And only those proffered experts who testified based on theories generally accepted by mainstream
professions from which their expertise was derived could offer opinions as
experts. Thus expansive or creative interpretation of the diagnostic nomenclature by an individual psychiatrist would not receive a sympathetic judicial reception.

Tort damage law through the first half of this century also proved in-
hospitable to claims for what is now diagnosed as PTSD. Whereas recovery
for tangible, physical injuries such as broken bones, lost wages, and damaged property sustained as the result of tortious conduct was available, recovery for nontangible, nonphysical harm alone was not. As was stated in
Lynch v. Knight (1861), "Mental pain or anxiety the law cannot value, and

does not pretend to redress, when the unlawful act complained of causes that alone" (p. 598).

Tort law posited, implicitly, a mind-body duality that recognized physical and mental harm as separate and distinct. Physical damage claims were thought to involve real injury and to be subject to objective diagnosis, but mental damage claims were not. Thus courts feared that fraud and malingering would not permit them to adjudicate these damage claims for nonphysical harm accurately, given the absence of accurate objective diagnostic criteria that they thought existed for physical injury. Courts also feared that if they permitted recovery for nonphysical harm they would be flooded with claims for bad manners and other minor annoyances that would be impracticable to administer. Moreover, courts fashioned rules based on the assumption that normal people were thick-skinned and did not suffer injury from fright (*Victorian Railway Commissioners v. Coultas* 1888). Feminist scholars explain this judicial reaction as valuing property and physical security, traditionally managed and owned by men, more highly than human relationships and emotional security, traditionally managed by women (Chamallas and Kerber 1990). This duality is interesting not only in light of current thinking in psychiatry that rejects a rigid mind-body duality (Goodman 1991) but also in terms of the brain pathology model explanation for disordered behavior that existed when these rules were formulated in the nineteenth century.

Consequentially, courts fashioned rules that limited recovery for nonphysical harm. These rules were hardly consistent, however. They permitted recovery for nonphysical harm in cases of intentional torts such as assault, battery, and false imprisonment because the number of these cases was thought to be smaller and the culpability of the defendant was regarded as greater, although the problems of valuation are no less difficult in these cases (Magruder 1936; Smith 1944). And courts later permitted recovery in cases of negligence when the nonphysical harm was parasitic to physical impact or injury, for example, pain and suffering that resulted from physical harm caused by the defendant's negligence. This action was thought to provide some assurance that the claims were not wholly fabricated or resulted from "ordinary commonsense reasoning" that physical trauma may have an emotional consequence (Perlin 1991). Claims for injuries now diagnosed as PTSD standing alone, however, were not then welcome in the courts.

The recognition of the diagnostic nomenclature for PTSD in 1980 in DSM-III (American Psychiatric Association 1980) and changes in the legal rules in the 1960s and 1970s heralded a new generation of litigation. PTSD sweeps much within its grasp. From combat stress (Atkinson 1982) to sexual assault (*Alphonso v. Charity Hospital* 1982), natural and man-made disasters (Newman 1976), automobile (*Johnson v. May* 1992) and industrial accidents (*Carter v. Gen. Motors* 1961), the stressors that could trigger PTSD and the class of victims who could suffer PTSD from those stressors expanded the horizons of tort litigation. Because the inclusion of PTSD in DSM-III was based on a consensus that "the stressor was the primary etiologic factor determining the symptoms that people develop in the setting of extreme adversity" (McFarlane 1990, p. 4) and does not imply a self-limiting disorder, PTSD implies an absence of blame or fault on the part of the victim that is more likely to gain the sympathy of a judge or jury. The current language of psychiatry facilitates PTSD claims.

The expansive reach of PTSD in DSM-III and, subsequently, in DSM-III-R (American Psychiatric Association 1987) set in motion another facet of PTSD litigation. Using the same diagnostic nomenclature for the responses of an expanded group of people to an expanded panoply of stressors raises the question whether all who suffer PTSD should be expected to respond similarly. Because neither DSM-III nor its successors, DSM-III-R and the recently published DSM-IV (American Psychiatric Association 1994), purport to distinguish the symptoms of PTSD in women who have been battered by a spouse (Walker 1976), for example, from the symptoms of PTSD in men who have witnessed relatives killed in a building collapse (Wilkinson 1983), a cottage industry of experts has developed to offer their services to litigants on these distinctions (Shuman 1989). And because the ability to convey technical information in a nontechnical fashion and to reach firm conclusions is often most important in jurors' evaluations of the believability of expert testimony (Champagne 1991), there is reason to doubt that the various syndromes accepted in court purporting to distinguish the symptoms of different categories of PTSD are supported by methodologically sound research.

Coincidental with the expansion of the diagnostic nomenclature, the judicial threshold for the admission of this evidence was lowered with the enactment of the Federal Rules of Evidence in 1974 and subsequently adopted state rules patterned after them. The rules reflected the opinion of many legal scholars, who viewed that their predecessors were overly restrictive and that this restrictiveness excluded a great deal of helpful testimony. Rather than risk exclusion of potentially helpful evidence, a shift in the rules of evidence occurred, which resulted in a bias in favor of admission of relevant evidence, absent countervailing considerations, leaving it to the jurors to choose between competing experts (*Barefoot v. Estelle* 1983).

At the same time, relevance, rather than general acceptance in the relevant professional community, gained support as the threshold for scrutinizing scientific evidence. Thus expansive or creative interpretation of the diagnostic nomenclature by an individual psychiatrist was more likely to receive a sympathetic judicial reception.

Concurrently, tort rules governing recovery for nonphysical harm became more malleable. Increasingly, proximate cause, rather than physical impact or injury, defined the limits on recovery for nonphysical harm (*Dillon v. Legg* 1968). *Proximate cause* is an enigmatic phrase that is most often thought to turn on foreseeability. Liability is limited to the foreseeable consequences that flow from an act (*Palsgraf v. Long Island R.R.* 1928). Even though the requirement of cause-in-fact is met, the defendant is only legally responsible for the foreseeable consequences of his or her actions. Although foreseeability is a prospective test to be applied from the perspective of the defendant at the time of the injury producing conduct, its application at trial is affected by hindsight bias.

Research on hindsight bias by cognitive psychologists reveals that people who know the outcome of an event view that outcome as more likely than people who have been asked to predict the occurrence without knowledge of its outcome (Fischoff 1975). Thus, for example, jurors asked to assess whether it is foreseeable that leaving a vacant apartment unsecured increases the likelihood that a young girl in the neighborhood will be raped by an assailant using the apartment as a secluded location, are more likely to view that occurrence as a foreseeable risk having been told how the rape occurred (*Nixon v. Mr. Property Management Co.* 1983). Civil trials are rarely bifurcated, and jurors are typically informed of the outcome of the event whose foreseeability they have been asked to predict. Accordingly, whereas proximate cause might initially have been considered as a limitation on the consequences of an event to which liability might attach, hindsight bias may result in it having the opposite effect (Wexler and Schopp 1991).

What the future holds for PTSD litigation is, like the past and present, a function of what occurs with the diagnostic nomenclature and the tort rules governing recovery for nonphysical harm. Because PTSD litigation turns, in part, on diagnostic nomenclature that psychiatry largely controls, psychiatry can influence the direction of PTSD litigation. There are at least two alternatives for the psychiatric profession to provide greater guidance and to exercise greater control over the diagnostic nomenclature for PTSD.

The first alternative is the issue of the nomenclature itself. Neither the DSM nor any other authoritative psychiatric source explicitly addresses legally relevant behavior. Are all who suffer PTSD expected to behave similarly? For example, does a rape trauma syndrome (Burgess 1983) exist for a subgroup of subjects with PTSD that accurately describes the behavior of women who have been sexually assaulted? Does that syndrome differ according to the age, ethnicity, or socioeconomic status of the woman assaulted, or the degree of physical violence involved? Does the syndrome also describe the behavior of men who have been sexually assaulted? Is rape trauma syndrome similar to or different from PTSD in people who have experienced different stressors? Is PTSD valid in children (Saigh 1989)? If so, can children who experience the same stressor as adults be expected to exhibit the same symptoms as adults?

These kinds of questions proliferate in the courts. And although the DSM raises these questions about legally relevant behavior through the use of broad diagnostic nomenclature, it offers little guidance in their resolution. Elsewhere, I (Shuman 1989) have argued that, either in the DSM or a separate document, the American Psychiatric Association should provide guidance to the courts in defining the boundaries of accepted professional knowledge about legally relevant behavior rather than leaving this to be defined in court on a case-by-case basis, often based on less than all the best, current research. This document might inform the courts, for example, whether a critical review of the literature yields a professional consensus that children who have been sexually abused respond similarly and, if so, what that similar behavior includes. When courts are proceeding without the boundaries of professional consensus, they would be alerted to be hypervigilant in their scrutiny of syndrome evidence purporting to describe common behavior of sexually abused children or some other PTSD group.

The second alternative involves the appropriate use of the nomenclature in individual cases. The DSM is not intended to be a forensic "cookbook" or a lay medical guide. Yet its diagnostic criteria are enticing to judges and lawyers as a lay guidebook to psychiatry for the unschooled and untrained. The Georgetown University practice standards for forensic evaluations offers to fill a gap in forensic practice left by the DSM and to provide significant guidance in the competence and procedures necessary for the appropriate use of the nomenclature in individual cases. There are a number of categorical concerns that the practice standards should address to aid in appropriate forensic application of the PTSD nomenclature: the competence of the evaluator, the establishment of the forensic relationship, the methods and procedures for the evaluation, the information used in the evaluation, and the presentation of the evaluation.

Qualification as an expert witness is not generic but rather issue specific. Licensure as a physician who practices psychiatry, or even board certification in psychiatry, should not, in and of itself, result in qualification as an expert on PTSD. Thus standards addressing competence to evaluate PTSD should go beyond articulating the basic qualifications to practice psychiatry. The practice standards should describe in detail the education, training, and experience appropriate to evaluate PTSD competently in specific cases. They should address common elements of competence to evaluate PTSD and any additional qualifications that may be appropriate for particular stressors (e.g., sexual assault) or particular persons (e.g., children) (see Quinn, Chapter 4, this volume). Although the practice standards would not be binding on the courts, they could provide useful guidance in retaining and appointing competent evaluators and challenging incompetent evaluators.

Interrelated with competence is the evaluator's capacity to apply the skill impartially. Even if an evaluator possesses the requisite education, training, and experience, he or she should not conduct an evaluation if other professional activities, personal views, or methods of compensation create conflicts that do not permit the evaluator to apply those skills impartially. One activity that conflicts with an impartial evaluation is providing therapy to the claimant. The roles of patient ally and impartial evaluator are inconsistent and risk unnecessary disclosure of confidential information. Therefore, a psychiatrist treating a claimant should not serve as a forensic examiner for that claimant (see Simon, Chapter 3, this volume).

Establishment of the forensic relationship for a PTSD evaluation raises no unique forensic issues. If a party is represented by counsel, counsel should be notified of the evaluation; if a party is not represented by counsel, the evaluator should not proceed with the evaluation until the party has had the opportunity to retain counsel. As in all forensic evaluations, the examiner should proceed only under the authority of a written court order or obtain the informed consent of the client or party (American Psychiatric Association 1984). In the absence of either, or when the evaluator has doubts about capacity to consent, the evaluator should seek clarification from the court and counsel before proceeding with the evaluation.

Judicial determinations are efforts to resolve uncertainty in proceedings in which life, liberty, and property hang in the balance. They are no place for antiquated or unproven modes of providing information that purport to be scientific. Thus the methods and procedures of the evaluation should be grounded in currently accepted clinical and scientific standards. The practice standards can serve an important function by informing the judiciary and the psychiatric profession of the currently accepted methods and procedures for the evaluation of PTSD. In setting forth these methods and procedures, the practice standards should be mindful of the importance of a multimethod-multitrait assessment (Grisso 1986) that addresses concerns with the reliability of information supplied by the client or party being evaluated (see Simon, Chapter 3, this volume).

The information used in the evaluation must be accurate and complete. Thus it should include at minimum 1) a detailed history of the event, its consequences to the claimant, changes in living patterns, and treatment efforts; 2) collateral information about the traumatic event, including witness statements and police reports, and interviews with family members; and 3) a psychiatric history, medical history, litigation history, and criminal record (see Resnick, Chapter 6, this volume; Simon, Chapter 3, this volume).

The information used in the evaluation must also be obtained in an appropriate manner. Before any evaluation proceeds, the examinee must be informed of the purpose and intended use of the evaluation, the methods that will be used, and who has retained or appointed the evaluator (Shuman 1994). The evaluator must also be familiar with the rules of evidence such as privilege and hearsay that may limit the sources of information legally available to the evaluator. Finally, the evaluator should be familiar with the limits on privilege or confidentiality of the evaluation and seek to keep confidential that which is not germane to the evaluation.

Presentation of the results of the evaluation should address the competence of the evaluator, the process used to establish the forensic relationship, the methods and procedures used in the evaluation, the information used in the evaluation, and the evaluator's findings and supporting reasoning. Because forensic evaluations are made with explicit knowledge of their intended use in an adversary setting in which the phrasing of a question or the tone of an answer are matters of great concern, evaluators are obligated to document accurately and to preserve completely the bases for their evaluation. This is particularly important in PTSD evaluations in which concerns with malingering and the reliability of information supplied by the client or party are widespread (Faust and Ziskin 1989). All tests or interviews should be preserved in the best manner available. When feasible, this may obligate forensic evaluators to consider videotaping evaluations (Weinstein 1991), although this may interject a new variable into the evaluation. An added advantage of videotaping evaluations is that it may alleviate the perceived necessity of many claimant's attorneys to be present during the evaluation, which evaluators also claim to taint the evaluation, when the attorney's concern is accurate reporting of the evaluation.

The possibility for significant change that may affect the future of PTSD litigation is not limited to psychiatric nomenclature. The legal winds of change whisper the words of that inscrutable sage Yogi Berra: It seems like "déjà vu all over again." At least at the federal level, the rules of evidence have been interpreted to require a more restrictive approach to the admissibility of expert testimony than had been taken at the time of their adoption 20 years ago (*Daubert v. Merrel Dow Pharmaceuticals* 1993). Federal judges have been instructed to scrutinize the scientific validity underlying expert testimony by taking into account, among other things, peer review and publication of the underlying theory or technique.

The expansion of tort law in the 1960s and 1970s that favored plaintiffs in personal injury litigation has generally stabilized (Henderson and Eisenberg 1992). Courts that had interpreted foreseeability expansively now interpret foreseeability more restrictively to limit the liability issues that may be presented to a jury. And because nonphysical harm is often the largest portion of damage awards in a personal injury litigation, and because it has no natural limits, tort reform efforts have targeted damages for nonphysical harm (Carroll 1987).

The challenge is to compensate those with PTSD fairly and accurately. It is by no means easily met. Indeed, it is a problem that invokes Loa Tzu's observation that "ruling a big kingdom is like cooking a small fish." The forensic practice standards are a well-considered opportunity for psychiatry to raise the level of forensic practice and the quality of psychiatric input in PTSD litigation.

References

Alphonso v Charity Hospital, 413 So2d 982 (La Ct App 1982)

American Psychiatric Association: Diagnostic and Statistical Manual of Mental Disorders, 3rd Edition. Washington, DC, American Psychiatric Association, 1980

American Psychiatric Association: Psychiatry in the Sentencing Process: A Report of the Task Force on the Role of Psychiatry in the Sentencing Process. Washington, DC, American Psychiatric Association, 1984

American Psychiatric Association: Diagnostic and Statistical Manual of Mental Disorders, 3rd Edition, Revised. Washington, DC, American Psychiatric Association, 1987

American Psychiatric Association: Diagnostic and Statistical Manual of Mental Disorders, 4th Edition. Washington, DC, American Psychiatric Association, 1994

Atkinson RM, Henderson RG, Sparr LF, et al: Assessment of Vietnam veterans for posttraumatic stress disorder in veterans administration disability claims. Am J Psychiatry 139:1118–1121, 1982

Barefoot v Estelle, 463 US 880, 898 (1983)

Burgess AW: Rape trauma syndrome. Behavioral Sciences and the Law 1:97–113, 1983

Carroll SJ: Assessing the Effects of Tort Reforms. Santa Monica, Ca, Rand, 1987

Carter v Gen Motors, 106 NW2d 361 (Mich 1961)

Chamallas M, Kerber LK: Women, mothers and the law of fright: a history. Michigan Law Review 88:814–864, 1990

Champagne A, Shuman D, Whitaker E: An empirical examination of the use of expert witnesses in American courts. Jurimetrics Journal 31:375–392, 1991

Daubert v Merrel Dow Pharmaceuticals, 113 S Ct 2786 (1993)

Dillon v Legg, 441 P2d 912 (Cal 1968)

Erichsen JE: On Concussion of the Spine. New York, W Woodward & Company, 1882

Goodman A: Organic unity theory: the mind-body problem revisited. Am J Psychiatry 148:553–563, 1991

Faust D, Ziskin J: Challenging post-traumatic stress disorder claims. Defense Law Journal 38:407–424, 1989

Fischoff B: Hindsight ≠ foresight, the effect of outcome knowledge on judgment of uncertainty. J Exp Psychol Hum Percept Perform 1:288–299, 1975

Grisso T: Psychological assessment in legal contexts, in Forensic Psychiatry and Psychology: Perspectives and Standards for Interdisciplinary Practice. Edited by Curran WJ, McGarry AL, Shah SA, et al. Philadelphia, PA, Davis, 1986, pp 103–128

Henderson J, Eisenberg T: Inside the quiet revolution in products liability. University of California at Los Angeles Law Review 39:731–810, 1992

Johnson v May, 585 NE2d (Ill App Ct 1992)

Lynch v Knight, 9 HL Cas 577, 598 (1861)

Magruder C: Mental and emotional disturbance in the law of torts. Harvard Law Review 49:1033–1067, 1936

McFarlane AL: Vulnerability to posttraumatic stress disorder, in Posttraumatic Stress Disorder: Etiology, Phenomenology, and Treatment. Washington, DC, American Psychiatric Press, 1990, pp 3–20

Mendelson G: The concept of posttraumatic stress disorder: a review. Int J Law Psychiatry 10:45–62, 1987

Modlin HC: Is there an assault syndrome? Bull Am Acad Psychiatry Law 13:139–145, 1985

Mott FW: Mental hygiene and shell shock. BMJ 2:39–42, 1917

Newman CJ: Children of disaster: clinical observations at buffalo creek. Am J Psychiatry 133:306–312, 1976

Nixon v Mr Property Management Co, 690 SW2d 546 (Tex 1983)

Palsgraf v Long Island RR, 162 NE 99 (NY 1928)

Perlin M: Pretextuality, psychiatry and law: of "ordinary common sense," heuristic reasoning, and cognitive dissonance. Bull Am Acad Psychiatry Law 19:131–150, 1991

Saigh PA: The validity of the DSM-III posttraumatic stress disorder classification as applied to children. J Abnorm Psychol 98:189–192, 1989

Shuman DW: Psychiatric and Psychological Evidence. Colorado Springs, CO, Shepard's/McGraw-Hill, 1986

Shuman DW: The Diagnostic and Statistical Manual of Mental Disorders in the courts. Bull Am Acad Psychiatry Law 17:25–32, 1989

Shuman DW: The use of empathy in forensic examinations. Ethics and Behavior 3:289–302, 1994

Smith H: Relation of emotions to injury and disease: legal liability for psychic stimuli. Virginia Law Review 30:193–317, 1944

Victorian Railway Commissioners v Coultas, LR 13 App Cas 22, 8 Eng Rul Cas 405-PC (1888)

Walker L: The Battered Woman. New York, Harper & Row, 1976

Weinstein JB: Rule 702 of the federal rules of evidence is sound: it should not be amended. Federal Rules Decisions 138:631–645, 1991

Wexler DB, Schopp RF: How and when to correct for juror hindsight bias in mental health malpractice litigation: some preliminary observation, in Essays in Therapeutic Jurisprudence. Edited by Wexler DB, Winick BJ. Durham, NC, Carolina Academic Press, 1991, pp 135–155

White JB: Heracles' Bow: Essays on the Rhetoric and Poetics of Law. Madison, WI, University of Wisconsin Press, 1985

Wilkinson CB: Aftermath of a disaster: the collapse of the Hyatt Regency Hotel skywalks. Am J Psychiatry 140:1134–1139, 1983

Recent Research Findings on the Diagnosis of Posttraumatic Stress Disorder

Prevalence, Course, Comorbidity, and Risk

Bonnie L. Green, Ph.D. —————————————————————

This chapter addresses recent research on posttraumatic stress disorder (PTSD) with regard to several issues, including epidemiology, course, comorbid psychopathology, and risk factors for the development of the disorder. Changes from DSM-III-R to DSM-IV (American Psychiatric Association 1987, 1994) are noted briefly, along with future research directions.

Epidemiology of Trauma in the General Population

Recent research has shown that up to three-quarters of the general population in the United States has been exposed to a traumatic event in their lifetimes that might meet the DSM stressor criterion for PTSD. Kilpatrick and Resnick (1993) found that 75% of a community sample of women reported at least one crime victimization, but most had multiple victimizations, including 24%–53% who reported a sexual assault. Koss et al. (1987) reported that 54% of over 3,800 college women nationwide reported experiencing some form of sexual victimization, the experiences of 15% qualifying legally as rape. In a national telephone survey reported by Finkelhor et al. (1990), childhood sexual abuse was reported by 27% of women and 16% of men. High rates of domestic violence, predominantly spouse and child abuse, have also been reported based on a national telephone survey (Straus and Gelles 1986), with severe abuse of children occurring at a yearly rate of about 11% and severe couple violence at about 6% yearly. Norris (1992), studying both men and women, queried a community sample of residents of four southeastern cities about their exposure to a variety of traumatic events (e.g., physical and sexual assault, tragic death, robbery, disaster, motor vehicle accidents with serious injury, fire, combat) and found a lifetime exposure rate to at least one event of 69%, with tragic death (via homicide, suicide, or accident; 30%), robbery (25%), and motor vehicle accidents with injury (23%) being reported most frequently.

The prevalence of these events varies from study to study, based on 1) the specific definitions of the events, 2) the population(s) studied, 3) whether questions are open ended or specific, and 4) whether the individual is interviewed by telephone or in person. Thus no absolute rates are available. Also, some of the events studied may not meet the DSM stressor criteria for PTSD for each individual. However, it is clear that exposure to "traumatic" events is common in the lifetime of individuals. Although quite a few of these individuals go on to develop PTSD symptoms from their exposure, many do not. The factors associated with the development of this syndrome are reviewed later in this chapter.

Rates of PTSD Following Traumatic Exposure

PTSD is not the only diagnosis that is associated with exposure to traumatic events. For example, major depression, alcohol abuse or dependence, drug abuse or dependence, and phobia diagnoses were all shown to be significantly higher (at least twice the rate) in general population respondents exposed to sexual assault compared with respondents who did not report sexual assault (Burnam et al. 1988). Further, studies have indicated an association of certain types of traumatic events (particularly childhood sexual abuse) with borderline personality disorder (e.g., Herman et al. 1989) and dissociative identity disorder (formerly called multiple personality disorder) (e.g., Braun 1990).

Because this chapter concerns PTSD, however, the focus will be on the findings with this diagnosis (although discussion follows on diagnostic comorbidity). Population studies of trauma and PTSD indicate that, on the average, about a quarter of individuals who are exposed to a DSM-IV *criterion A* type event go on to develop the full-blown PTSD syndrome. In the Kilpatrick and Resnick (1993) study mentioned earlier, 39% of the women who had experienced aggravated assault developed PTSD, as did 35% of those who were raped. Of those who experienced traumatic bereavement, 25% developed PTSD, along with 23% of those who were molested as children.

In Breslau et al.'s (1991) study of young adults in Detroit, life threat, seeing others killed or badly injured, and physical assault all produced lifetime PTSD rates of around 25%. Accident victims showed PTSD rates of 12%; however, rape victims reported a PTSD lifetime prevalence of 80%. This rate is similar to that from a recent study by Rothbaum et al. (1992), who found an initial (2-week) rate of PTSD following rape to be 94%. Breslau et al. estimated the lifetime prevalence of PTSD in the general population to be 9%.

Norris (1992) studied current symptoms of PTSD, which were gathered from questionnaire items. The recency of these events varied across the study. Norris estimated *current* rates of PTSD to be 14% from sexual assault, 13% from physical assault, 12% from motor vehicle accidents, 5% from disaster, and 8% from tragic death. Therefore, Norris estimated rates of PTSD in individuals exposed to traumatic events as ranging from 5% to 11%. These rates are similar to those in the Kilpatrick and Resnick (1993) study of crime victims, who showed current PTSD rates of 12% from sexual assault, 13% from rape, 5% from traumatic bereavement, and 2% from sexual molestation.

PTSD rates in male Vietnam combat veterans from a recent national study (Kulka et al. 1990) were shown to be 31% lifetime and 15% current. For women, the figures were 27% lifetime and 9% current (Fairbank et al., in press). The same study estimated current rates of PTSD in nonveterans to be 1.2% in men and only 0.3% among women.

PTSD Comorbidity With Other Diagnoses

PTSD is rarely found alone, even in community samples. A recent review of this literature (Green et al. 1992) indicated that in patient samples of Vietnam War veterans that have been studied from this perspective, over three-quarters of patients with PTSD also met criteria for a least one other diagnosis (e.g., Keane and Wolfe 1990). The most common coexisting diagnoses in these samples are major depression and substance abuse. In a community sample of veterans (Kulka et al. 1990), 73% of subjects with current PTSD also met criteria for substance abuse, whereas 26% met criteria for major depression. Antisocial personality disorder was also fairly common (31% of those with PTSD) in this population.

Little research has been done on nonveteran populations. Kilpatrick et al. (1987; reported in Keane and Wolfe 1990) found that of community crime victims with PTSD, 41% also reported sexual dysfunction, 32% had major depressive disorder, 27% had obsessive-compulsive disorder, and 18% had phobias.

We (Green et al. 1992) compared a community sample of disaster survivors to a community sample of Vietnam War veterans. Although both groups were in their second decade posttrauma, they differed in many ways, including age, gender mix, trauma type, cultural characteristics, and instruments used to assess the disorders. However, their diagnostic profiles were quite similar. The base rates for PTSD were similar between the two groups (29% for veterans, 25% for disaster survivors), and PTSD was the most common diagnosis in both groups. Less than 6% of the individuals in each group had PTSD alone. The most common concurrent diagnoses with PTSD for both groups were major depressive disorder, phobic disorder, and generalized anxiety disorder (GAD). Substance abuse was less common overall but more common in veterans than disaster survivors. Joint prevalence of PTSD with each other separate disorder was under 20% in each sample, indicating that with which diagnoses co-occurred varied among individuals. However, 42% of individuals with PTSD in the disaster sample also had major depressive disorder, 42% had GAD, and 30% had phobia. Antisocial personality disorder was virtually nonexistent in the disaster survivor sample, although it was 11% in the veteran sample, suggesting that age and sex may play a role in the symptom picture.

Our study (Green et al. 1992) was not able to determine why such comorbidity exists. Potential reasons offered by investigators in the field include that the symptom/diagnostic criteria overlap, that the pattern of comorbidity may be related to the specific nature of the stressor or to historic or genetic factors, or that the other diagnoses result from (are a reaction to) the PTSD. All of these explanations have some empirical support, but little research exists to sort out one possibility compared with another.

Comorbidity is a complex issue and is likely determined by multiple factors. However, it seems clear that clients claiming PTSD are also likely to have other DSM diagnoses, particularly anxiety and depression disorders, and possible substance abuse, although the latter diagnoses may be more common in certain subpopulations. Therefore, presence of these diagnoses should not necessarily be seen as weakening the case for PTSD.

Longitudinal Studies of PTSD

Little research has been done on the longitudinal course of PTSD; however, the research that exists suggests that it may be a very long-lasting disorder without treatment intervention. Several studies that have used structured interviews to assess the lifetime and current prevalence of PTSD in certain survivor groups provide indirect information about the longitudinal course of the disorder. This indirect information is derived from estimates of the proportion of survivors developing the disorder in the first place who continue to have it at some point, often years, later. The national Vietnam War veteran study (Kulka et al. 1990) just noted was of this type and indicated that 31% of the male sample reportedly had combat-related PTSD at some point. Half of these subjects (15%) continued to meet full criteria 20 years or so after the war. For women, the comparable figures were 27% and 9%, respectively. A study of World War II POWs (Speed et al. 1989) showed a lifetime rate of 50% and a current rate of 29%, again suggesting that up to half of those individuals who develop the disorder may still have it decades later.

Kilpatrick and Resnick (1993), in their crime victim study, showed a somewhat lower proportion of current, compared with lifetime, PTSD in their sample, ranging from about one-third for assault and rape survivors to 20% for traumatic bereavement and to only 9% for sexual molestation.

A few studies have examined the longitudinal course of PTSD prospectively. Rothbaum et al. (1992), and Rothbaum and Foa (1993), studied a general sample of rape victims referred by police, emergency rooms, and mental health professionals. At 2 weeks, as noted previously, 94% of these 95 individuals met full PTSD criteria. By 1 month, the current rate was 65%, at 2 months it was 53%, and at 3 months it was 47%. A 9-month follow-up showed the same rate (47%) as at 3 months. This group of investigators also did a similar study of nonsexual criminal assault (including robbery), finding 65% exhibiting PTSD at 1 week, 37% at 1 month, 25% at 2 months, and 12% at 6 months. At 9 months, none of the victims had PTSD. The fact that the rates differed in these two studies was not explained by the authors but may have been due to the nature of the event.

A study of children by Nader et al. (1990) showed that 77% of the children who were present during a playground sniper attack showed severe or moderate PTSD at 1 month. At 14 months, 74% of the children still had PTSD. Children who were more removed from the attack tended to recover over this same period.

Solomon et al. (1989) studied Israeli combat veterans who had and had not experienced combat stress reactions (CSRs) during the Lebanon war over a 3-year period. As might be expected, soldiers who developed CSRs during battle were much more likely to develop PTSD in the subsequent 3 years (63% versus 14% at 1 year). However, tracking both groups, the authors found some decrease, but not a dramatic one, in rates of PTSD over time. The rates at 1, 2, and 3 years for the CSR veterans were 63%, 57%, and 43%, respectively. For the non-CSR veterans, the figures were 14%, 17%, and 9%, respectively.

Looking at how PTSD reactions might influence medical variables, Holen (1990, 1991) studied the insurance records of Norwegian oil workers who survived an oil rig collapse in the North Sea. Most of those on board died, and many of the survivors witnessed the deaths of their co-workers. The records of another group of Norwegian oil rig workers not in a collapse also were studied. Records of both groups were reviewed from 2 years before the incident to 8 years after it. As expected, the two groups differed significantly on almost all symptoms of PTSD. Particularly striking, however, were the data on sick leave and health problems in the survivors. Although there were no differences in use of sick leave prior to the event, the traumatized group, after the incident, had twice as many episodes of sick leave as the control subjects, and the mean number of weeks of leave was four times higher in the survivors. This effect continued throughout the 8 years of study and was accounted for primarily by psychiatric problems and by subsequent accidents.

Thus there is clear evidence that PTSD is a long lasting disorder in many individuals. Up to half of those who develop the disorder may continue to have it decades later without treatment. On the other hand, the rates of PTSD usually decline over time, indicating that some cases do remit.

There is much less information regarding the severity of the disorder over time. In a study (Green et al. 1990b) of survivors of a dam collapse, we investigated the symptoms of PTSD/stress response. These data were collected in the context of a lawsuit at 2 years, whereas follow-up at 14 years was done without this context and included both litigants and nonlitigants. The rate of "probable PTSD" (PTSD was not a diagnosis in 1974 when the first study was done; however, symptoms of "traumatic neurosis" and "gross stress reaction" were gathered systematically) decreased from 44% to 28%

over 12 years, consistent with findings from other studies. It was interesting to note that the severity of the impairment associated with PTSD declined as well. The average global severity rating, considering all symptoms and functioning, decreased from 3.9 (moderate) in 1974 to 2.7 (mild) in 1986, suggesting that those individuals who had the diagnosis, on average, were less impaired at 14 years than they were at 2 years.

Most longitudinal studies not specifically measuring PTSD show these trends as well, although findings seem to relate to type of event. For example, in a recent comprehensive review of the disaster literature (Green and Solomon, in press), several longitudinal studies were found. Among the studies of *natural disasters,* particularly those with better samples/designs and/or multiple assessments on the same person, reports tended to show a drop-off of symptoms in general community samples by 1–3 years. *Technological disasters,* however, showed effects that were more prolonged, although not many studies with long-term follow-up were found. These studies tended to show a decrease in symptoms as well but not to "normal" levels. In technological events, there is even some evidence that symptoms falling under the category of anger/irritability may increase over time. These technological events probably have more in common with suits that are brought to court than do natural disasters.

Thus the course of PTSD symptoms, particularly in human-caused events, seems to be a decrease over time without treatment but not necessarily to normal levels. Even the prognosis with treatment, particularly with chronic disorders, may be guarded, although the studies that have been done have all examined short-term or pharmacologic interventions. For example, although a study by Kosten et al. (1991) showed phenelzine to be superior to imipramine and placebo in treating intrusion symptoms in combat veterans with PTSD, only 44% of the phenelzine patients showed improvement on the Impact of Event Scale. A study of amitriptyline by Davidson et al. (1990) showed that 64% of the treated sample still met criteria for PTSD at the end of (8 weeks of) treatment. Brom et al. (1989) found clinical improvement in 60% of their patients treated for PTSD with desensitization or hypnosis or psychodynamic treatment (average 15 sessions), but they found improvement in only 26% of untreated patients. In a study by Foa et al. (1991), 50% of rape victims treated with stress inoculation and 40% of those treated with exposure no longer had PTSD at the end of treatment. Supportive-counseling and waiting-list patients nearly all continued to meet criteria for PTSD. Thus although studies have generally found treatment to be effective, relatively speaking, about half of those treated may still meet full criteria for PTSD at termination, suggesting that this disorder may be relatively refractory to (short-term) treatment. (For a recent review of controlled treatment trials for PTSD, see Solomon et al. 1992.)

Individual Differences Among Who Develops PTSD

Stressor Severity

The primary risk factor that has been associated empirically with the development of PTSD is the level or severity of exposure to stressors. Vietnam War veterans have been the group most widely studied with regard to etiology, although the severe and prolonged nature of their stressor experience, and their age and sex, may not be typical of cases that find their way into the courts. However, this literature is important to include when evaluating risk factors, and the findings from this group do tend to generalize to other groups as well. Several reviews (Fairbank et al., in press; Foy et al. 1987; March 1993) have indicated that most studies of Vietnam War veterans have found level of exposure (to combat and to abusive violence) to be associated with higher rates of PTSD. Premilitary factors have also been shown to predict PTSD, however, usually at a lower level. March (1993) reviewed 19 studies that quantified stressors suffered during combat, disaster, illness, injury, and crime, and found that in 16 of 19 studies examining the question of stressor intensity, a dose-response relationship between stressor intensity and outcome was found.

In a study examining the genetic contribution to the development of PTSD in Vietnam War veterans, Goldberg et al. (1990) compared the prevalence of PTSD in male monozygotic twins, one of whom served in Vietnam and one of whom did not. That study found a strong effect of exposure to combat. Further study of this group (True et al., in press), however, showed that, more specifically, the intrusive symptoms of PTSD were related to level of combat, whereas the numbing symptoms showed much lower relationships with combat and were more strongly explained by genetic factors.

None of these studies identified a threshold effect. The threshold notion does pose some problems for the PTSD diagnosis in that severity of stressors is conceptually a continuum (Breslau and Davis 1987). A few studies have attempted to examine "ordinary" stressors to determine whether they can produce PTSD. Burstein (1985) found that 8 of 73 patients in an outpatient setting met symptom criteria for PTSD without meeting the stressor criterion. Events associated with PTSD symptoms in these individuals included marital disruption, children's illegal activities, and death of a loved one. The Epidemiologic Catchment Area studies in St. Louis (Helzer et al. 1987) found that a spouse's affair, miscarriage, and poisoning were associated with PTSD, although less commonly than more severe stressors. Solomon and Canino (1990) found that PTSD symptoms, particularly reexperiencing, were more prevalent in persons experiencing common events (e.g., money problems, injury) than in those who had been in a natural disaster.

With regard to the type of stressor, a variety of types of events have been associated with the development of PTSD: injury, violent or unexpected bereavement, witnessing or participating in abusive violence, exposure to grotesque death, hearing about the death of another person, life threat, rape, and torture (Green 1990, March 1993). Most studies do find these associations, but a few do not. Injury (extent of) is one type of event that does not have consistent findings regarding its association with PTSD. However, most of these studies were of combat veterans, and therefore the independent effects of injury are difficult to parcel out. Even so, a number of investigators have found that extent of objective physical injury is not necessarily the best predictor of outcome (Landsman et al. 1990; Malt 1988; Malt et al. 1989). Perceived loss of function may play a greater role.

Other Risk Factors

The national Vietnam War veteran's readjustment study (Kulka et al. 1990) mentioned earlier used a national probability sample of over 1,500 Vietnam veterans. This study examined a large range of potential risk factors for the development of PTSD. As noted previously, the strongest risk factor was combat exposure. However, a number of other variables were also shown to predict PTSD. These included socioeconomic status while growing up, psychiatric symptoms prior to exposure, and reported childhood abuse. Our own study of Vietnam War veterans (Green et al. 1990a) showed that having a prior (to service) Axis I diagnosis and young age at the time of service were significant predictors of combat-related PTSD in the second decade postwar. However, these prewar factors explained only half as much variance in the PTSD diagnosis as did exposure to war stressors. Further, these stressors "explained" the diagnosis of PTSD much more than they did other diagnoses that were sometimes associated with PTSD in this community sample.

A community study of a variety of types of stressors (Breslau et al. 1991) identified several risk factors for both exposure to traumatic events and the development of PTSD after exposure to a traumatic event. Exposure was associated with low education, male sex, early conduct problems, extraversion, and family history of psychiatric disorders or substance abuse. Risk factors for PTSD after exposure to a traumatic event included female sex, early separation from parents, neuroticism, preexisting anxiety or depression, and family history of anxiety or antisocial behavior. A recent study (Resnick et al. 1992) of crime victims in the community did *not* show an association between a precrime Axis I diagnosis and PTSD after crime. However, the study did find an interaction in which the rate of PTSD was associated with prior depression in the high crime-stress exposure group but not in the low exposure group. They concluded that precrime depression may constitute a vulnerability factor for development of PTSD under conditions of exposure to high crime stress.

The community study by Norris (1992) also showed women to be more vulnerable to PTSD after exposure to a traumatic event. This study found younger, rather than elderly, subjects to be at higher risk for PTSD, a finding in line with other studies. Findings regarding race have been mixed in this and other studies.

In the review of disaster research studies mentioned earlier (Green and Solomon, in press), I found, as did March (1993), that nearly all of the studies that examined exposure intensity showed that level of exposure predicted outcome (not always PTSD). The bulk of studies also showed that women were more at risk for stress symptoms after both natural and technological disaster and that the impact of age is most likely curvilinear, with middle-aged individuals most at risk. Most studies also indicated that prior psychiatric problems increased the risk for postdisaster symptoms, as did prior disaster experience (Green, in press).

A few studies in the literature have been prospective; however, the large-sample community studies referred to because of their comprehensiveness and nonbiased nature are essentially retrospective. That is, the person is recalling symptoms that he or she had prior to the target event. It can be argued that it may not be that individuals with prior psychiatric problems are more likely to develop PTSD, but that individuals who currently suffer from PTSD are more likely to recall earlier symptoms. Further, almost no studies have examined persons' exposure to prior traumatic events. Yet there is increasing evidence that exposure to multiple events is more common than previously thought and that prior traumatic exposure increases the risk for the development of PTSD following the target event (e.g., Fairbank et al. 1993; Kramer and Green 1991). This area is being explored increasingly and should add considerably to our understanding of vulnerability to PTSD.

Field Trials and DSM-IV

The following comments on DSM criteria are made from my perspective as a member of the advisory committees for PTSD for both DSM-III-R and DSM-IV of the American Psychiatric Association. The draft criteria for DSM-IV were published in March 1993, and the final DSM-IV was published in mid-1994. The following comments share some of the progress that led to the draft.

With regard to overall philosophy, the DSM-IV committee decided that changes would not be made in the current nosology unless there was compelling research evidence supporting that change. That perspective dictated few dramatic changes in the criteria for the various disorders. However, several changes were proposed for the PTSD diagnosis. The most debate regarding this diagnosis concerned two issues. One was the definition of the stressor criterion. The other, actually tangential to PTSD but relating to trauma, was whether there should be additional diagnoses that reflect responses to traumatic events. Further, our committee conducted a large research study (D. G. Kilpatrick et al., unpublished observations, 1992) to investigate these issues and made recommendations based on that trial. The following is a summary of the findings from the trial and the issues discussed.

Briefly, there were concerns raised about the definition of the stressor in DSM-III-R, primarily because studies since its publication have demonstrated that a number of the traumatic stressors that were considered likely to lead to PTSD were not, in fact, "outside of the range of normal human experience." A good example is sexual assault, which, unfortunately, as just indicated, is not uncommon. The original proposals regarding the changing of the stressor criterion ranged from tightening up the DSM-III-R version to eliminating the criterion altogether and letting anyone with the symptom criteria receive the diagnosis. Although the second option is, in some ways, more appropriate for research because it allows those events that lead to the disorder to be defined empirically, it may be less useful for clinical practice and may be too broad for forensic settings in which any event, regardless of how minor, could be claimed to produce PTSD. Numerous definitions were proposed, with differences focusing on how to define the stressor objectively, how to make the definition as compatible as possible with the ICD-10 (the international classification system with which there have been attempts to collaborate around similarities of classification), and, finally, whether the definition should include an additional requirement that the event was subjectively experienced in a particular way.

These considerations, along with the empirical results from the field trial, were debated and discussed. The field trial (Dean Kilpatrick, Ph.D., principal investigator) was conducted at five sites, and it included 128 individuals from the community and 400 patients. Individuals were interviewed regarding demographic characteristics, high- and low-magnitude event stressors, symptoms of PTSD, and symptoms of disorder of extreme stress not otherwise specified (DESNOS) (discussion follows).

The field trial investigated five different options for the definition of the stressor in the PTSD section, including eliminating the definition altogether. As it turned out, these varied definitions had very little effect on the variation in prevalence rates for PTSD (less than 3% difference from one definition to the next). Few people developed PTSD symptoms unless they had experienced extremely stressful events (i.e., high-magnitude stressors, as defined in this study). The field trial investigators thus proposed a simple definition, clarified in the text, that focused on the individual's definition of the event as stressful (Kilpatrick et al. 1992). However, further discussion with the larger anxiety disorders and DSM-IV committees raised concerns that this definition would be too loose and particularly were concerned about legal ramifications of too broad a definition. Thus the final proposal (Davidson and Foa 1992) for DSM-IV was to adopt a definition that required that "the person experienced, witnessed, or was confronted with an event or events that involved actual or threatened death or serious injury, or a threat to the physical integrity of self or others" *and* "the person's response involved intense fear, helplessness, or horror" (American Psychiatric Association 1994, pp. 427–428). The text is clear that childhood sexual abuse that has taken place in the absence of threatened or actual physical violence or injury also may produce PTSD. The text indicates that the event(s) can involve direct personal experience, witnessing, or learning about such events. Life-threatening illness is specifically mentioned as a criterion A stressor in the text.

Few changes in the symptoms themselves were recommended. Physiologic reactivity at exposure to reminders was moved from the arousal section (D) to the reexperiencing section (B). A few wording changes were also made. The symptom duration required remained at more than 1 month, and acute and chronic subtypes are demarcated at 3 months. *Delayed* is a subtype, with a 6-month qualifying period. New to the criteria is the requirement that the disturbance causes clinically significant distress or impairment in social, occupational, or other important areas of functioning.

Summary and Research Directions

Recent research indicates that traumatic events, when defined using objective criteria, are relatively common in the general population. Although PTSD is not the only diagnosis that has been linked to exposure to traumatic events, in studies that have examined a variety of diagnoses, it is usually the most common. Other diagnoses that have been associated with trauma include major depression, substance abuse, phobia, and panic. Furthermore, studies of patient populations link trauma with borderline and dissociative personality disorders, eating disorders, and somatization disorders. It is not clear whether these other (particularly Axis I) disorders are produced directly from exposure to the trauma or stem more from living with the chronic condition of PTSD, but anxiety and depression diagnoses, in particular, are often comorbid with PTSD. The personality disorders are usually assumed to result from repeated traumatic exposure in childhood, but research specifically addressing this assumption is sparse.

Rates of PTSD given exposure average around 25% in the general population, although certain types of exposure, for example rape, routinely produce much higher rates. Those who develop PTSD may maintain it for long periods of time, over decades, without treatment intervention. A number of studies have shown that up to half of individuals with PTSD may continue to have it for many years. Even many patients treated for PTSD, in short-term treatment, may continue to meet full criteria for the diagnosis at termination. On the other hand, prevalence rates do decrease over time, even without treatment intervention, and, for some types of events, may virtually be reduced to zero. Much more research is needed to define this area. With regard to severity, average levels of symptoms decline in groups of exposed individuals over time. It is not known whether this is because all individuals show some symptom reduction or whether some individuals become symptom free, whereas others maintain high levels of distress. One study showed that severity of functioning was reduced over a 12-year period, on average, even in those individuals who continued to meet full diagnostic criteria. Conversely, another study showed maintenance of indicators of dysfunction (sick leave) over an 8-year period, with no decrease.

Development of PTSD has been clearly linked with level of exposure to objective aspects of the stressor experience, usually in a dose-response fashion. Thus intensity of exposure is a clear-cut risk factor for the development of PTSD. Other risk factors, noted in several studies, are low education/social class, preexisting psychiatric symptoms or diagnoses, prior trauma, and a family history of psychiatric problems. Women are usually shown to be more at risk as well.

The definition of PTSD, both with regard to the stressor criterion and with regard to symptoms, changed very little with the publication of DSM-IV. The field trial for the disorder showed that people rarely develop PTSD without exposure to highly stressful events as presently defined in the criteria.

Ongoing research is addressing several areas. One is the impact of multiple exposure to traumatic events. Prior research has focused primarily on one target event without assessing exposure to prior traumas. Yet recent findings indicate that exposure to multiple events increases the risk for PTSD. More longitudinal studies are also being conducted, attempting to recruit subjects early and trace the waxing and waning of symptoms over time. A few studies of disaster have fortuitously been able to obtain prospective data by virtue of having conducted epidemiologic studies in an area that later experiences a disaster. Data are then available before and after the event. A few recent studies have begun to compare different types of events with each other to determine differences and similarities in outcomes (not just PTSD) across event type. A number of investigators have also begun to examine life-threatening illness (e.g., cancer) from a trauma or PTSD perspective.

Biological studies of trauma and PTSD are also becoming more common (see Pitman 1993, and Ver Ellen and van Kammen 1990 for reviews of this literature). These include biological studies of autonomic responses, neuroregulatory processes, endocrine function, and sleep studies. These studies have supported both tonic and phasic symptoms of PTSD. Such studies are attempting to differentiate PTSD from other disorders and hope to suggest pharmacologic treatments that would be efficacious. More studies are needed in the area of treatment interventions for this disorder.

References

American Psychiatric Association: Diagnostic and Statistical Manual of Mental Disorders, 3rd Edition, Revised. Washington, DC, American Psychiatric Association, 1987

American Psychiatric Association: Diagnostic and Statistical Manual of Mental Disorders, 4th Edition. Washington, DC, American Psychiatric Association, 1994

Braun BG: Dissociative disorders as sequelae to incest, in Incest-Related Syndromes of Adult Psychopathology. Edited by Kluft RP. Washington, DC, American Psychiatric Press, 1990, pp 227–245

Breslau N, Davis GC, Andreski P, et al: Traumatic events and posttraumatic stress disorder in an urban population of young adults. Arch Gen Psychiatry 48:216–222, 1991

Breslau N, Davis GC: Posttraumatic stress disorder: the stressor criterion. J Nerv Ment Dis 175:255–264, 1987

Brom D, Kleber RJ, Defares PB: Brief psychotherapy for posttraumatic stress disorders. J Consult Clin Psychol 57:607–612, 1989

Burnam MA, Stein JA, Golding JM, et al: Sexual assault and mental disorders in a community population. J Consult Clin Psychol 56:843–850, 1988

Burstein A: Posttraumatic stress disorder (letter). J Clin Psychiatry 46:554, 1985

Davidson J, Kudler H, Smith R, et al: Treatment of posttraumatic stress disorder with amitriptyline and placebo. Arch Gen Psychiatry 47:259–266, 1990

Fairbank JA, Schlenger WE, Caddell JM, et al: Post-traumatic stress disorder, in Comprehensive Handbook of Psychopathology, 2nd Edition. Edited by Sutker PB, Adams HE. New York, Plenum, 1993

Finkelhor D, Hotaling G, Lewis IA, et al: Sexual abuse in a national survey of adult men and women: prevalence, characteristics, and risk factors. Child Abuse Negl 14:19–28, 1990

Foa EB, Rothbaum BO, Riggs DS, et al: Treatment of posttraumatic stress disorder in rape victims: a comparison between cognitive-behavioral procedures and counseling. J Consult Clin Psychol 59:715–723, 1991

Foy D, Sipprelle R, Ruger D, et al: Etiology of posttraumatic stress disorder in Vietnam veterans: analysis of premilitary, military and combat exposure influences. J Consult Clin Psychol 43:643–649, 1987

Goldberg J, True WR, Eisen SA, et al: A twin study of the effects of the Vietnam War on posttraumatic stress disorder. JAMA 263:1227–1232, 1990

Green BL: Defining trauma: terminology and generic stressor dimensions. Journal of Applied Social Psychology 20:1632–1642, 1990

Green BL: Traumatic stress and disaster: mental health effects and factors influencing adaptation, in International Review of Psychiatry, Vol 2. Edited by Liehmak F, Nadelson C. Washington, DC, American Psychiatric Press (in press)

Green BL, Solomon SD: The mental health impact of natural and technological disasters, in Traumatic Stress: From Theory to Practice. Edited by Freedy JR, Hobfoll SE. New York, Plenum (in press)

Green BL, Grace MC, Lindy JD, et al: Risk factors for PTSD and other diagnoses in a general sample of Vietnam veterans. Am J Psychiatry 147:729–733, 1990a

Green BL, Lindy JD, Grace MC, et al: Buffalo Creek survivors in the second decade: stability of stress symptoms. Am J Orthopsychiatry 60:43–54, 1990b

Green BL, Lindy JD, Grace MC, et al: Chronic posttraumatic stress disorder and diagnostic comorbidity in a disaster sample. J Nerv Ment Dis 180:760–766, 1992

Helzer J, Robins L, McEvoy L: PTSD in the general population. N Engl J Med 317:1630–1634, 1987

Herman JL, Perry JC, van der Kolk BA: Childhood trauma in borderline personality disorder. Am J Psychiatry 146:490–495, 1989

Holen A: A Long-Term Outcome Study of Survivors From a Disaster. Unpublished doctoral dissertation, University of Oslo, Oslo, Norway, 1990

Holen A: A longitudinal study of the occurrence and persistence of post-traumatic health problems in disaster survivors. Stress Medicine 7:11–17, 1991

Keane T, Wolfe J: Comorbidity in posttraumatic stress disorder: an analysis of community and clinical studies. Journal of Applied Social Psychology 20:1776–1788, 1990

Kilpatrick D, Saunders B, Veronen L, et al: Criminal Victimization: Lifetime Prevalence, Reporting to Police, and Psychological Impact. Paper presented at the meeting of the Association for the Advancement of Behavior Therapy, Boston, MA, November, 1987

Kilpatrick DG, Resnick HS: PTSD associated with exposure to criminal victimization in clinical and community populations, in Posttraumatic Stress Disorder: DSM-IV and Beyond. Edited by Davidson JRT, Foa EB. Washington, DC, American Psychiatric Press, 1993, pp 113–143

Koss MP, Gidycz CA, Wisniewski N: The scope of rape: incidence and prevalence of sexual aggression and victimization in a national sample of higher education students. J Consult Clin Psychol 55:162–170, 1987

Kosten TR, Frank JB, Dan E, et al: Pharmacotherapy for posttraumatic stress disorder using phenelzine or imipramine. J Nerv Ment Dis 179:366–370, 1991

Kramer TL, Green BL: Posttraumatic stress disorder as an early response to sexual assault. Journal of Interpersonal Violence 6:160–173, 1991

Kulka RA, Schlenger WE, Fairbank JA, et al: Trauma and the Vietnam War Generation. New York, Brunner/Mazel, 1990

Landsman IS, Baum CG, Arnkoff DB, et al: The psychosocial consequences of traumatic injury. J Behav Med 13:561–581, 1990

Malt U: The long-term psychiatric consequences of accidental injury. Br J Psychiatry 153:810–818, 1988

Malt UF, Blikra G, Hoivik B: The three-year biopsychosocial outcome of 551 hospitalized accidentally injured adults. Acta Psychiatr Scand Suppl 355:84–93, 1989

March JS: What constitutes a stressor? The "Criterion A" issue, in Posttraumatic Stress Disorder: DSM-IV and Beyond. Edited by Davidson JRT, Foa EB. Washington, DC, American Psychiatric Press, 1993, pp 37–54

Nader K, Pynoos R, Fairbanks L, et al: Children's PTSD reactions one year after a sniper attack on their school. Am J Psychiatry 147:1526–1530, 1990

Norris FH: Epidemiology of trauma: frequency and impact of different potentially traumatic events on different demographic groups. J Consult Clin Psychol 60:409–418, 1992

Pitman RK: Biological findings in posttraumatic stress disorder: implications for DSM-IV classification, in Posttraumatic Stress Disorder: DSM-IV and Beyond. Edited by Davidson JRT, Foa EB. Washington, DC, American Psychiatric Press, 1993, pp 173–189

Resnick HS, Kilpatrick DG, Best CL, et al: Vulnerability—stress factors in development of posttraumatic stress disorder. J Nerv Ment Dis 180:424–430, 1992

Rothbaum BO, Foa EB, Riggs DS, et al: A prospective examination of post-traumatic stress disorder in rape victims. Journal of Traumatic Stress 5:455–475, 1992

Rothbaum BO, Foa EB: Subtypes of posttraumatic stress disorder and duration of symptoms, in Posttraumatic Stress Disorder: DSM-IV and Beyond. Edited by Davidson JRT, Foa EB. Washington, DC, American Psychiatric Press, 1993, pp 23–35

Solomon S, Canino G: Appropriateness of the DSM-III-R criteria for post-traumatic stress disorder. Compr Psychiatry 31:227–237, 1990

Solomon SD, Gerrity ET, Muff AM: Efficacy of treatments for posttraumatic stress disorder. JAMA 268:633–638, 1992

Solomon Z: Psychological sequelae of war: a 3-year prospective study of Israeli combat stress reaction casualties. J Nerv Ment Dis 177:342–346, 1989

Speed N, Engdahl B, Schwartz J, et al: Post-traumatic stress disorder as a consequence of the POW experience. J Nerv Ment Dis 177:147–153, 1989

Straus MA, Gelles RJ: Societal change and change in family violence from 1975–1985 as revealed by two national surveys. Journal of Marriage and the Family 48:465–479, 1986

True WR, Rice J, Eisen SA, et al: A twin study of genetic and environmental contributions to liability for posttraumatic stress symptoms. Arch Gen Psychiatry 50:257–264, 1993

Ver Ellen P, van Kammen D: The biological findings in post-traumatic stress disorder: a review. Journal of Applied Social Psychology 20:1789–1821, 1990

Toward the Development of Guidelines in the Forensic Psychiatric Examination of Posttraumatic Stress Disorder Claimants

Robert I. Simon, M.D.

Four out of every 10 Americans have been exposed to a major traumatic event by the age of 30 (Davidson 1991). Posttraumatic stress disorder (PTSD) develops in one-quarter of the trauma-exposed population, making it the most common preventable major mental illness. Moreover, a significant increase in suicide, drug abuse, and other psychiatric disorders is associated with PTSD. Chronic physical conditions, including hypertension, peptic ulcers, and bronchial asthma, also have a higher coexistence with the diagnosis of PTSD.

With litigation burgeoning, PTSD has become a growth industry. As Stone (1993) observes, "No diagnosis in the history of American psychiatry has had a more dramatic and pervasive impact on law and social justice than posttraumatic stress disorder" (p. 23). Traditionally, PTSD has been applied to personal injury claims based on the psychological consequences of automobile and public carrier accidents, home and industrial accidents, and mass disasters. A few notable examples of mass disasters include the Buffalo Creek flood in West Virginia, the collapse of the Hyatt Regency Hotel skywalk in Kansas City, the Three Mile Island nuclear accident, and war-related injuries of the Vietnam War and previous wars. Currently, in litigation, PTSD is being alleged as a consequence of all kinds of accidents and human mishaps (Slovenko 1994).

In the criminal law, defendants have pleaded not guilty by reason of insanity secondary to PTSD (Sparr 1990). The diagnosis of PTSD has been alleged in criminal proceedings by prosecutors to bolster the credibility of the victim or by experts who attempt to argue backward from PTSD symptoms to establish the occurrence of a traumatic stressor (e.g., rape). Victims of criminal acts who develop PTSD or other psychiatric disorders may sue under criminal injuries compensation acts. PTSD has bolstered the advocates of "victim rights" whose advocacy poses a threat to the constitutional rights of defendants (Stone 1993).

A study by Appelbaum et al. (1993) found that, contrary to concerns, PTSD was associated infrequently with an insanity defense. A PTSD diagnosis was no more likely to succeed than any other diagnosis and differed little from other insanity defendants. The fear that PTSD would be widely misused in connection with the insanity defense was not corroborated.

A brief history of PTSD reveals that, in an earlier incarnation, it was diagnosed as *railway spine* in the nineteenth century. Such injuries were particularly common with the burgeoning of railroads. It was thought that concussion of the spine with concomitant injury to the sympathetic nervous system caused the observed traumatic neurosis (Trimble 1981). In World War I and II, traumatic stress disorders were called variously *shell shock, battle fatigue, traumatic neurosis,* and *the concentration camp syndrome.* With the advent of the DSM (American Psychiatric Association 1952), the disorder was labeled *gross stress reaction.* In DSM-II (American Psychiatric Association 1968), it was named *adjustment reaction of adult life.* Finally, with the publication of DSM-III (American Psychiatric Association 1980), the diagnosis of PTSD was created. In DSM-IV (American Psychiatric Association 1994), PTSD underwent further modification in diagnostic criteria.

The Forensic Evaluation

There are five standard questions that the forensic examiner should ask regarding every PTSD claim:

1. Does the alleged PTSD claim actually meet specific clinical criteria for this disorder?
2. Is the traumatic stressor that is alleged to have caused the PTSD of sufficient severity to produce this disorder?

3. What is the preincident psychiatric history of the claimant?
4. Is the diagnosis of PTSD based solely on the subjective reporting of symptoms by the claimant?
5. What is the claimant's *actual* level of functional psychiatric impairment?

Each question will be explored and guidelines proposed for the forensic psychiatric examination of the PTSD claimant. The proposed guidelines are not intended to be proscriptive. Rather, these guidelines provide reasonable clinical latitude for performing a credible forensic examination (see Table 3–1). The importance of clinical experience and sound judgment is presumed and, therefore, not explicitly stated within the proposed guidelines.

Table 3–1. Proposed guidelines for the forensic psychiatric examination of posttraumatic stress disorder (PTSD) litigants

---

1. In evaluating the diagnostic criteria for PTSD, the forensic examiner should be guided by official diagnostic manuals, the professional literature, and current research. Idiosyncratic definitions of PTSD must be avoided. If official diagnostic criteria are not used, the burden of proof should be on the forensic examiner to provide the scientific evidence for his or her diagnosis of PTSD.
2. In assessing the sufficiency of traumatic stressors for the diagnosis of PTSD, the forensic examiner should be guided by official diagnostic manuals, the professional literature, and current research. The possible contributions of multiple stressors to the PTSD claimant's clinical picture should be evaluated.
3. A credible forensic psychiatric evaluation of a PTSD claimant requires a thorough examination of the claimant's psychiatric and medical history, including review of prior medical, psychiatric, and other pertinent records.
4. Relying solely on the subjective reporting of symptoms by the PTSD claimant without considering additional sources of information is insufficient. As a corollary, treater and forensic roles should not be mixed in the forensic examination of the PTSD claimant.
5. Standard assessment methods should be used in evaluating the level of functional psychological impairment of PTSD claimants. Relying solely on clinical experience or on strictly subjective or idiosyncratic criteria in assessing psychological impairment should be avoided.

Diagnostic Criteria for PTSD

PTSD, perhaps more than any other psychiatric disorder, is defined by certain psychological symptoms unique only to this disorder. In the DSM-III-R (American Psychiatric Association 1987), PTSD is defined according to specific stressor (criterion A) and symptom criteria (criteria B, C, and D) (see Table 3–2). In DSM-IV, minor yet significant changes were made to the stressor and symptom criteria (see Tables 3–3 and 3–4). Repeated reexperiencing of the traumatic event, either through recurrent nightmares; distressing, intrusive recollections; or flashback experiences, is the hallmark feature of PTSD (criterion B). Symptom 4 of criterion B, "intense psychological distress at exposure to events that symbolize or resemble an aspect of the traumatic event . . ." (American Psychiatric Association 1987, p. 250), occurs in a number of psychiatric disorders. DSM-IV adds exposure to "internal" cues as a source of "intense psychological distress" (American Psychiatric Association 1994, p. 428). Yet, symptom 4 in both DSM-III-R and DSM-IV does not appear to be specific enough, by itself, to be considered a hallmark symptom of PTSD.

Flashbacks are an essential part of the *total* symptom picture in PTSD. Flashbacks that exist by themselves may be found among well-adjusted people, however, and are not, per se, evidence of organic or functional psychopathology (Spiegel 1991). Moreover, flashbacks may be a manifestation of normal memory and attention processes (McGee 1984).

In addition to the hallmark symptoms of PTSD (criterion B), DSM-III-R and DSM-IV specify other criteria necessary to make the diagnosis of PTSD (i.e., "persistent avoidance of stimuli associated with the trauma or numbing of general responsiveness" and "persistent symptoms of increased arousal" [criteria C and D] [American Psychiatric Association 1987, p. 250; 1994, p. 428]). Unlike the hallmark reexperiencing of symptoms of criterion B, symptoms in criteria C and D are not unique to PTSD but are symptoms that may overlap with other psychiatric disorders. For example, in criterion C, *numbing* phenomena are specified, including detachment from others, loss of interest in life events, loss of ability to feel or experience normal emotions, and a sense of a foreshortened future. Combined with the criterion D symptoms of sleeplessness, difficulty concentrating, anger, and hostility, this complex of symptoms becomes very difficult to distinguish from symptoms of depression.

In delayed PTSD, reexperiencing symptoms may develop months (greater than 6 months) or years after the trauma. Avoidance symptoms (criterion C) usually have been present, however, from the time of trauma

---

Table 3–2. DSM-III-R criteria for posttraumatic stress disorder (PTSD)

A. The person has experienced an event that is outside the range of usual human experience and that would be markedly distressing to almost anyone, e.g., serious threat to one's life or physical integrity; serious threat or harm to one's children, spouse, or other close relatives and friends; sudden destruction of one's home or community; or seeing another person who has recently been, or is being, seriously injured or killed as a result of an accident or physical violence.

B. The traumatic event is persistently reexperienced in at least one of the following ways:
   (1) recurrent and intrusive distressing recollections of the event (in young children, repetitive play in which themes or aspects of the trauma are expressed)
   (2) recurrent distressing dreams of the event
   (3) sudden acting or feeling as if the traumatic event were recurring (includes a sense of reliving the experience, illusions, hallucinations, and dissociative [flashback] episodes, even those that occur upon awakening or when intoxicated)
   (4) intense psychological distress at exposure to events that symbolize or resemble an aspect of the traumatic event, including anniversaries of the trauma

C. Persistent avoidance of stimuli associated with the trauma or numbing of general responsiveness (not present before the trauma), as indicated by at least three of the following:
   (1) efforts to avoid thoughts of feelings associated with the trauma
   (2) efforts to avoid activities or situations that arouse recollections of the trauma
   (3) inability to recall an important aspect of the trauma (psychogenic amnesia)
   (4) markedly diminished interest in significant activities (in young children, loss of recently acquired developmental skills such as toilet training or language skills)
   (5) feeling of detachment or estrangement from others
   (6) restricted range of affect, e.g., unable to have loving feelings
   (7) sense of a foreshortened future, e.g., does not expect to have a career, marriage, or children, or a long life

D. Persistent symptoms of increased arousal (not present before the trauma), as indicated by at least two of the following:
   (1) difficulty falling or staying asleep
   (2) irritability or outbursts of anger
   (3) difficulty concentrating
   (4) hypervigilance

Table 3–2.   DSM-III-R criteria for posttraumatic stress disorder (PTSD)
                 (continued)

   (5) exaggerated startle response
   (6) physiologic reactivity upon exposure to events that symbolize or resemble
       an aspect of the traumatic event (e.g., a woman who was raped in an ele-
       vator breaks out in a sweat when entering any elevator)
   E. Duration of the disturbance (symptoms in B, C, and D) of at least one month.
Specify delayed onset if the onset of symptom was at least six months after
the trauma.

Source.   Reprinted with permission from American Psychiatric Association:
Diagnostic and Statistical Manual of Mental Disorders, 3rd Edition, Revised.
Washington, DC, American Psychiatric Association, 1987. Copyright 1987,
American Psychiatric Association.

in delayed PTSD (DSM-III-R: PTSD, Delayed Onset; American Psychiatric
Association 1987, p. 251). Here, the forensic examiner must be careful to
rule out the occurrence of a subsequent, unrelated traumatic stressor as
the proximate cause of the alleged delayed PTSD. PTSD symptoms of less
than 1 month duration are very common but do not meet the duration
criteria for this disorder. In DSM-IV, the diagnosis of acute stress disorder
is made in persons with PTSD who have dissociative symptoms lasting between a minimum of 2 days and a maximum of 4 weeks beginning within 4
weeks of the traumatic event (see Table 3–5). A proposal was made but
rejected to extend the 1-month criteria to 3 months in DSM-IV to curtail
overdiagnosing PTSD (Rothbaum and Foa 1993). The diagnosis of chronic
PTSD was dropped from DSM-III-R but was added to DSM-IV if the duration of symptoms is 3 months or more. A diagnosis of acute PTSD is made
if the duration of symptoms is less than 3 months. In DSM-IV, clinicians are
encouraged to consider specific culture and age features that influence the
diagnosis of PTSD among traumatized immigrants and younger children.

   Unless the criteria sufficient for the diagnosis of PTSD are present, the
basis for the claimant's diagnosis of PTSD is not valid. It is not unusual
when investigating a claim of PTSD to find that the clinical criteria for a
PTSD diagnosis are not fulfilled. Instead, one may find either the continu-
ation of unrelated, chronic Axis I (clinical syndromes) or Axis II (personality disorders) conditions, their exacerbation, or the development of new
but totally different psychiatric conditions.

   Forensic examiners must be careful not to overreach in order to diag-

Table 3–3. DSM-IV criteria for posttraumatic stress disorder (PTSD)

A. The person has been exposed to a traumatic event in which both of the following were present:
   (1) the person experienced, witnessed, or was confronted with an event or events that involved actual or threatened death or serious injury, or a threat to the physical integrity of self or others
   (2) the person's response involved intense fear, helplessness, or horror. **Note:** In children, this may be expressed instead by disorganized or agitated behavior
B. The traumatic event is persistently reexperienced in at least one (or more) of the following ways:
   (1) recurrent and intrusive distressing recollections of the event, including images, thoughts, or perceptions. **Note:** In young children, repetitive play may occur in which themes or aspects of the trauma are expressed.
   (2) recurrent distressing dreams of the event. **Note:** In children, there may be frightening dreams without recognizable content.
   (3) acting or feeling as if the traumatic event were recurring (includes a sense of reliving the experience, illusions, hallucinations, and dissociative flashback episodes, including those that occur on awakening or when intoxicated). **Note:** In young children, trauma-specific reenactment may occur.
   (4) intense psychological distress at exposure to internal or external cues that symbolize or resemble an aspect of the traumatic event
   (5) physiological reactivity on exposure to internal or external cues that symbolize or resemble an aspect of the traumatic event
C. Persistent avoidance of stimuli associated with the trauma and numbing of general responsiveness (not present before the trauma), as indicated by three (or more) of the following:
   (1) efforts to avoid thoughts, feelings, or conversations associated with the trauma
   (2) efforts to avoid activities, places, or people that arouse recollections of the trauma
   (3) inability to recall an important aspect of the trauma
   (4) markedly diminished interest or participation in significant activities
   (5) feeling of detachment or estrangement from others
   (6) restricted range of affect (e.g., unable to have loving feelings)
   (7) sense of a foreshortened future (e.g., does not expect to have a career, marriage, children, or a normal life span)
D. Persistent symptoms of increased arousal (not present before the trauma), as indicated by two (or more) of the following:
   (1) difficulty falling or staying asleep
   (2) irritability or outbursts of anger

Table 3–3.   DSM-IV criteria for posttraumatic stress disorder (PTSD)
                 (continued)

    (3) difficulty concentrating

    (4) hypervigilance

    (5) exaggerated startle response

E. Duration of the disturbance (symptoms in Criteria B, C, and D) is more than
    1 month.

F. The disturbance causes clinically significant distress or impairment in social,
    occupational, or other important areas of functioning.

Specify if:

    Acute: if duration of symptoms is less than 3 months

    Chronic: if duration of symptoms is 3 months or more

Specify if:

    With Delayed Onset: onset of symptoms at least 6 months after the stressor

Source. Reprinted with permission from American Psychiatric Association:
Diagnostic and Statistical Manual of Mental Disorders, 4th Edition. Washington, DC,
American Psychiatric Association, 1994. Copyright 1994, American Psychiatric
Association.

nose PTSD. Claimants who have experienced a significant trauma may not
necessarily develop PTSD. There may be other disorders that are both related and unrelated to the traumatic stressor in question, and those should
be diagnosed. For example, Davidson (1993) notes the existence of 10
trauma-related disorders other than PTSD found in DSM-III-R: brief reactive psychosis, multiple personality disorder (now called *dissociative identity
disorder* in DSM-IV), dissociative fugue, dissociative amnesia, conversion disorder, depersonalization disorder, dream anxiety disorder, somatization
disorder, borderline personality disorder, and antisocial personality disorder. Credibility is severely compromised when an examiner attempts to
force the diagnosis of PTSD when the criteria for this disorder clearly are
not fulfilled. If only a few PTSD criteria are met, a diagnosis of anxiety
disorder not otherwise specified may be appropriate. Because PTSD is incident specific, it has been a favorite diagnosis in litigation because it creates a presumption of causation. When other psychiatric disorders are
diagnosed, legal causation may be much more difficult to prove. Multiple
psychosocial stressors unrelated to the legal cause of action may be opera-
tive in producing the psychiatric disorder.

Other options should be considered when symptoms of PTSD do not rise to a level sufficient to meet DSM-III-R or DSM-IV criteria for PTSD diagnosis. Based on clinical judgment and experience, the examiner may conclude that the claimant's existing symptomatology is of sufficient severity to nevertheless support a PTSD diagnosis. On the other hand, the examiner may decide to merely describe the existing symptoms while clearly stating that DSM criteria are not met fully for PTSD. The examiner may conclude that the claimant is suffering from a posttraumatic stress syndrome, which is not an official DSM-III-R or DSM-IV diagnosis (Blank 1993). Moreover, some of the symptoms of a claimant's PTSD may resolve over time, thus no longer meeting the parsimonious criteria for diagnosis of this disorder.

Table 3–4. Summary of main PTSD criteria changes in DSM-IV (noted in italics)

Criterion A

Deleted: *. . . outside the range of normal human experience . . .*

Added: *. . . the person's response involved intense fear, helplessness, or horror . . .*

Criterion B

(1) Added: recollections of the event . . . *including images, thoughts, or perceptions . . .*

(4) Changed: . . . intense psychological distress at exposure to *events* to *internal or external cues . . .*

(5) Changed: . . . physiological reactivity on exposure to *events* to *internal and external* cues . . .

Moved from Criterion D to Criterion B

Criterion C

Changed: Persistent avoidance of stimuli associated with the trauma *and* numbing of general responsiveness . . . [*and* changed from *or*]

(1) Added: efforts to avoid . . . *conversations associated with the trauma*

(2) Added: efforts to avoid . . . *places or people*

(4) Added: markedly diminished . . . *participation in significant activities*

Criterion F

Added: *The disturbance causes clinically significant distress or impairment in social, occupational, or other important areas of functioning*

Specifiers

Added: *Acute* and *chronic*

Table 3–5. DSM-IV criteria for acute stress disorder

A. The person has been exposed to a traumatic event in which both of the following were present:
  (1) the person has experienced, witnessed, or was confronted with an event or events that involved actual or threatened death or serious injury, or a threat to the physical integrity of self or others
  (2) the person's response involved intense fear, helplessness, or horror
B. Either while experiencing or after experiencing the distressing event, the individual has three (or more) of the following dissociative symptoms:
  (1) a subjective sense of numbing, detachment, or absence of emotional responsiveness
  (2) a reduction in awareness of his or her surroundings (e.g., "being in a daze")
  (3) derealization
  (4) depersonalization
  (5) dissociative amnesia (i.e., inability to recall an important aspect of the trauma)
C. The traumatic event is persistently reexperienced in at least one of the following ways: recurrent images, thoughts, dreams, illusions, flashback episodes, or a sense of reliving the experience; or distress on exposure to reminders of the traumatic event.
D. Marked avoidance of stimuli that arouse recollections of the trauma (e.g., thoughts, feelings, conversations, activities, places, people).
E. Marked symptoms of anxiety or increased arousal (e.g., difficulty sleeping, irritability, poor concentration, hypervigilance, exaggerated startle response, motor restlessness).
F. The disturbance causes clinically significant distress or impairment in social, occupational, or other important areas of functioning or impairs the individual's ability to pursue some necessary task, such as obtaining necessary assistance or mobilizing personal resources by telling family members about the traumatic experience.
G. The disturbance lasts for a minimum of 2 days and a maximum of 4 weeks and occurs within 4 weeks of the traumatic event.
H. The disturbance is not due to the direct physiological effects of a substance (e.g., a drug of abuse, a medication) or a general medical condition, is not better accounted for by Brief Psychotic Disorder, and is not merely an exacerbation of a preexisting Axis I or Axis II disorder.

Source. Reprinted with permission from American Psychiatric Association: *Diagnostic and Statistical Manual of Mental Disorders,* 4th Edition. Washington, DC, American Psychiatric Association, 1994. Copyright 1994, American Psychiatric Association.

A cautionary clinical comment is necessary concerning the absence of PTSD symptoms at the time of examination and the phasic aspect of this disorder. Generally, clinicians have observed that patients experience alternating dominant phases or cycles of hyperarousal/intrusion and numbing/constriction (Horowitz 1976). When the cycles are long in duration, a delayed PTSD may be appropriately diagnosed. The presence of severe avoidant symptoms may mask the diagnosis of PTSD (Epstein 1993). Pitman (1993) states that PTSD consists of a combination of bimodal tonic and phasic features. Tonic features are manifested by the patient all or most of the time. Phasic features only manifest from time to time, usually when evoked by salient environmental stressors. This psychological model parallels Selye's (1950) biophysiological general adaptation syndrome that follows three stages: 1) alarm, 2) resistance, and 3) exhaustion when bodily resources have been depleted. It may be, however, that hyperarousal/intrusion symptoms are the direct result of the traumatic stressor, whereas the numbing denial symptoms are a defense or reaction to the primary symptoms of PTSD.

Other factors may contribute to missing the diagnosis of PTSD. False negatives may arise when a person denies symptoms of PTSD because of shame and the stigmatizing effect of PTSD, particularly when combined with litigation. Also, cultural differences may cause the forensic examiner to overlook the diagnosis of PTSD. The response to severe traumatic events does exhibit some universal features. Nevertheless, ethnocultural factors can play an important part in the person's susceptibility to PTSD as well as in the expression of PTSD symptoms and response to treatment (Marsella et al. 1993)

Hyperarousal-intrusive symptoms include hyperactivity, explosive violent outbursts, increased startle response, and unbidden recollections in the form of nightmares, flashbacks, and reenactment of the traumatic experience. Numbing-constriction symptoms involve denial, social isolation, emotional constriction and withdrawal, avoidance of family responsibilities, anhedonia (loss of pleasure), and estrangement from others. Thus the forensic examiner must inquire about *all* PTSD symptoms that have occurred, not merely the current symptoms described by the claimant. Otherwise, an incomplete clinical picture may be obtained, causing the diagnosis of PTSD to be missed.

Misinterpreting PTSD symptoms can be another cause for diagnostic error. PTSD, although classified as an anxiety disorder, is dominated by dissociative symptoms. Evidence is accumulating that a link exists between trauma and dissociative symptoms. Studies have shown that veterans with

PTSD are more hypnotizable than normal control subjects (Spiegel 1991). Dissociative processes are a prominent component of the response to trauma (Spiegel and Cardeña 1990). For example, reexperiencing phenomena are essentially dissociative in that they involve some disturbances or alteration in memory or consciousness. PTSD reexperiencing symptoms occur in a hierarchy from intrusive imagery to major dissociative enactments in which contact with contemporary reality and orientation is lost (Lowenstein 1991a). Blank (1985) has identified four types of intrusive recall in PTSD: vivid dreams and nightmares of traumatic events; remaining under the influence of vivid dream content after awakening, with difficulty in making contact with reality; conscious flashbacks experienced as intrusive, vivid hallucinations (any or all of the senses) with or without loss of contact with reality; and unconscious flashbacks felt as sudden, discrete experiences leading to actions that repeat or re-create a traumatic event. Awareness that a connection exists between the action and the past traumatic event is absent.

Reexperiencing phenomena involve recurrent, intrusive, distressing, often visual reexperiencing of the traumatic event. The claimant, for example, may describe a depersonalization event in which he or she sees and relives the traumatic event in graphic, vivid detail as if watching a movie. Thus merely thinking or reflecting anxiously about the traumatic event usually is not sufficient to meet reexperiencing criteria. Most often, it is the reexperiencing of feelings associated with traumatic events, not the contents of the memories per se, that persons with PTSD find so excruciating. Generally, the more dissociative the quality of the reexperiencing phenomenon described by the claimant, the more likely it solidly meets the hallmark criterion B for PTSD. From a treatment perspective, the magnitude of the acute dissociative response has important prognostic significance, requiring early and effective intervention (Davidson et al. 1989).

Short-term memory deficits have been described in persons diagnosed with PTSD (Bremner et al. 1993b). In claimants alleging PTSD and mild head injury, an overlapping of symptoms may occur (see Table 3–6). For example, the forensic examiner must be careful to distinguish the cognitive impairments of PTSD (difficulty concentrating and selective psychogenic amnesia) from cognitive impairment secondary to mild traumatic brain injury and the postconcussive syndrome. As a rule, postconcussive symptoms, including memory problems, start immediately after the injury and improve over the next few months. PTSD symptoms, however, may become more evident or may manifest a delayed onset (McAllister 1994). The loss of memory in PTSD usually involves only a circumscribed aspect of the

Table 3–6. Symptoms of postconcussive syndrome and criteria for posttraumatic stress disorder

Posttraumatic stress disorder	Postconcussive syndrome
Reexperiencing trauma	
Recurrent intrusive recollections of traumatic event	
Recurrent distressing dreams of traumatic event	
Flashbacks of traumatic event	
Intense distress triggered by symbolic reminders[a]	
Physiologic reactivity upon exposure to events resembling trauma	Hypochondriacal concerns Headache Dizziness
Avoidance	
Efforts to avoid thoughts or feelings associated with event	
Efforts to avoid activities that arouse event	
Inability to recall aspect of event (psychogenic amnesia)[a]	Memory deficits[a]
Markedly diminished interest in activities	Fatigue
Feelings of detachment	
Restricted range of affect	
A sense of foreshortened future	
Increased arousal	
	Increased sensitivity to noise[a] Photophobia
Difficulty falling or staying asleep[a]	Insomnia[a]
Irritability or outbursts of anger[a]	Irritability[a]
Difficulty concentrating[a]	Decreased concentration[a]
Hypervigilance	
Exaggerated startle response[a]	Anxiety[a]

[a]Symptoms and criteria that overlap between postconcussive syndrome and posttraumatic stress disorder.
Source. Reprinted with permission from Epstein RS, Ursano RJ: "Anxiety Disorders," in *Neuropsychiatry of Traumatic Brain Injury.* Edited by Silver JM, Yudofsky SC, Hales RE. Washington, DC, American Psychiatric Press, 1994, p. 293. Copyright 1994, American Psychiatric Press.

traumatic event, usually the most psychologically painful part. In amnesia secondary to head injury, memory is lost for the entire traumatic event, including some time before and after the head injury (retrograde and anterograde amnesia). When PTSD and head injury are alleged to occur together, it is a grave error to confound the cognitive impairments of PTSD with those of a brain injury. Each disorder must be investigated separately and thoroughly.

Finally, some of the reexperiencing symptoms are more resistant to distortion over time than others. For example, flashback symptoms tend to replay the trauma with visual fidelity over long periods of time. The intensity of the flashback, however, may diminish. On the other hand, recurrent nightmares manifest distortion of the traumatic event in the dream content within days to a few weeks. Nightmares occur throughout the sleep cycle. Recurrent posttraumatic nightmares during REM sleep recapitulate the trauma theme but rarely play back the traumatic incident in exact detail. Although the evidence is not conclusive, posttraumatic nightmares occurring earlier during stage II and stage III sleep usually preserve exact movie-like (eidetic) re-creations of the traumatic experience (van der Kolk et al. 1984). Nevertheless, because a certain degree of distortion of dream content occurring later during REM sleep is inevitable, malingering should be considered in claimants who report recurrent dreams months later that review the traumatic event in exact detail throughout the sleep cycle.

Should forensic examiners be required to follow DSM-III-R and DSM-IV criteria exclusively in making the diagnoses of PTSD? Do these criteria define PTSD symptoms too narrowly? Generally, the answer to the first question is yes. The answer to the second question is maybe. One study (Schottenfeld and Cullen 1985), for example, asserts that a somatoform version of this disorder exists and is often missed. Other PTSD variants not reported in DSM-III-R or DSM-IV include posttraumatic depression (Davidson and Fairbanks 1993); posttraumatic stress syndrome (Blank 1993) (when full criteria are not met); and the sequelae of prolonged and repeated trauma, referred to as disorder of extreme stress not otherwise specified (Herman 1993).

Courts have been divided on requiring the use of DSM criteria (Simon 1988). The California Workers' Compensation rating system requires the use of DSM diagnoses (Enelow 1991). Attorneys, because they lack clinical perspective, often approach DSM-III-R and DSM-IV in a formalistic and literal fashion. Under "Caveats in the Use of DSM-IV," the manual clearly warns, "It is important that DSM-IV not be applied mechanically by untrained individuals. The specific diagnostic criteria included in DSM-IV are meant to serve as guidelines to be informed by clinical judgment and are not meant to be used in a cookbook fashion" (p. xxiii).

DSM-III-R and DSM-IV criteria reflect the "prototypical case" with a certain diagnostic latitude for cases that are less clearly defined (Frances 1990). Persons sharing a diagnosis are likely to be heterogeneous, differing clinically in important ways. Symptoms also may overlap with a number of other diagnostic categories. In the clinical setting, DSM-III-R and DSM-IV possess important clinical utility in assisting diagnosis and treatment.

DSM-III-R and DSM-IV are the best clinical diagnostic instruments we have to date for PTSD. Both provide clear-cut operational definitions for the stressor criterion in PTSD while adding new information about primary and secondary symptomatology found in a wider range of populations (Wolfe and Keane 1990). In addition, the DSM-III-R and DSM-IV multiaxial system provides a comprehensive approach to psychiatric evaluation. It has gained acceptance in the mental health community and among forensic experts (Scrignar 1988, pp. 211–213). In California, a retired judge who presided over the Los Angeles Workers' Compensation Appeals Board emphatically stated, "Accordingly, for the legal system, the DSM-III-R was a heaven-sent aid to achieving an effective degree of uniformity and objectivity for evaluating psychiatric claims" (qtd. in Lasky 1991, p. 19). He went on to state that although DSM-III-R may not be totally accurate and needs improvement, this does not negate its utility as a practical aid in resolving disputes.

Construct and discriminant validity studies of PTSD (diagnostic criteria accurately define the disorder and distinguish it from other disorders) are evolving rapidly (Wolfe and Keane 1990). Reliability (interrater agreement) studies for DSM-III have been conducted by the National Institute of Mental Health (NIMH) in a series of field trials (American Psychiatric Association 1980, pp. 467–472). Davidson et al. (1989) demonstrated high interrater and test-retest reliability for DSM-III criteria for PTSD. In unpublished data, Davidson found that the new items included in DSM-III-R also showed excellent agreement (discussed in Davidson et al. 1989).

PTSD is classified under anxiety disorders in DSM-III-R and DSM-IV. The coefficients of agreements have been quite good for anxiety disorders (American Psychiatric Association 1980, pp. 470, 471) for phase I and II of field trials, respectively. NIMH-sponsored field trials for DSM-IV were run specifically for the diagnosis of PTSD (American Psychiatric Association Task Force on DSM-IV 1991, pp. H:15–H:19). Moreover, the laborious and painstakingly careful work done by competent researchers and clinicians working through 26 advisory committees in establishing the diagnostic cri-

teria for psychiatric disorders gives DSM-III-R and DSM-IV substantial credibility.

Both DSM-III-R and DSM-IV, however, carry clear cautionary statements concerning the relevancy limitations of this manual in legal settings.
Nevertheless, these DSM caveats do not negate the considerable value in
assessing the litigant along all five axes. Perr (1988) notes that the misuse
of the PTSD in litigation is striking, often bearing no relationship to the
requirements of the current diagnostic system. A clear example of the misuse of DSM-III-R and DSM-IV occurs when the psychiatrically uninformed
attorney approaches diagnostic criteria as if he or she were reading a statute. DSM-III-R and DSM-IV can be wittingly or unwittingly distorted in the
course of litigation to serve the purposes of one side or the other.

Some attorneys, for example, cloak the DSM in the trappings of absolute authority, tending to view DSM-III-R and DSM-IV diagnostic criteria as
"black letter law." Often overlooked is the fact that the DSM reflects a consensus about the classification and diagnosis at the time of publication.
Increased understanding of the mental disorders occurs as new knowledge
is generated by clinical experience and research. Attorneys lack the training, skill, and experience to appreciate the protean clinical presentations
of a disorder within the prototypical criteria described in the DSM. Moreover, specific diagnostic criteria for each mental disorder are offered only
as guidelines to clinicians for making diagnoses. When DSM criteria are
read like a statute, they rarely fit real-life patients. Lawyers should seek competent clinical assistance when using the DSM so as not to misuse it in the
legal context.

However, the alternative to using DSM criteria for PTSD is the reliance
on highly variable or even idiosyncratic PTSD criteria established according to the clinical biases and legal agendas of some forensic examiners.
Unfortunately, the standard criteria for the diagnosis of PTSD are ignored
by a significant number of mental health practitioners who enter the legal
arena. Juries and judges are frequently confused by the babel of testimony
presented concerning what is and what is not PTSD. Testimony that lacks
a scientific basis undermines the credibility of the testifier as well as that of
his or her profession. The ensuing harm done to claimants as well as defendants can be enormous.

The following clinical vignette illustrates the peril of ignoring basic
criteria in the diagnosis of PTSD:

> A 38-year-old male claimant suffers multiple arm and leg fractures during
> an airplane crash. Loss of consciousness for approximately 10 minutes

occurs, with significant retrograde and anterograde amnesia. The claimant's memory is continuous only up to the time of arrival at the airport. The claimant has a prior history of brief psychiatric treatment for generalized anxiety that was resolved. On one occasion, the claimant returns to view the site of the accident with his family. At the time of trial, the claimant's expert asserts that the claimant likely suffers PTSD secondary to the catastrophic trauma of the airplane crash. However, no reexperiencing, avoidance, or numbing symptoms are noted in the examination conducted by the claimant's experts months after the accident. Symptoms of moderate anxiety and depression are present. The claimant's expert asserts that delayed PTSD will eventually emerge, given the catastrophic nature of the traumatic stressor. The expert's testimony is severely undercut on cross examination when forced to admit that since no memory for the plane crash exists, no PTSD can develop from the accident itself.

The vignette illustrates that improbable testimony can result from an expert's attempt to overreach the clinical data. Some forensic examiners disregard or run fast and loose with established clinical criteria to arrive at a spurious diagnosis of PTSD. No symptom criteria for PTSD were manifested by the claimant in the clinical vignette. It is likely that the claimant suffered from an adjustment disorder with mixed emotional features or the recrudescence of the former anxiety disorder. On the other hand, Epstein (1993) reports a case in which the diagnosis of PTSD was missed because it was mistakenly believed that the patient had been unconscious during the accident.

Although a person may be unconscious during an extremely traumatic event, PTSD symptoms may nevertheless develop. The person may regain consciousness in a hospital to find that heroic emergency efforts are being administered and that his or her life is in peril. The subsequent PTSD symptoms reflect the events surrounding the resuscitation rather than the original traumatic event.

Proposed Guideline

In evaluating the diagnostic criteria for PTSD, the forensic examiner should be guided by official diagnostic manuals, the professional literature, and current research. Idiosyncratic definitions of PTSD must be avoided. If official diagnostic criteria are not used, the burden of proof should be on the forensic examiner to provide the scientific evidence for his or her diagnosis of PTSD.

Evaluating the Traumatic Stressor

The professional literature clearly demonstrates that the stressor *dose* is a major risk factor in the development of PTSD, determined in part by life threat, physical injury, object loss, and, in part, by the grotesqueness of the traumatic event (March 1993). Thus the *initial* traumatic psychological response is predicated on the severity of the stressor. The subsequent adaptional response varies according to the psychological meaning of the experience rather than the precise nature of the traumatic event. The definition of the traumatic event is of critical importance to the diagnosis of PTSD. This criterion (criterion A) in DSM-III-R and DSM-IV serves as the gatekeeper to the diagnosis of PTSD (Davidson and Foa 1991).

According to DSM-III-R, the symptoms of PTSD develop after one experiences a psychologically stressful event that is outside the range of usual human experience (e.g., natural disasters, rape, torture). The traumatic stressor is expected to be markedly distressing to almost any person, though not necessarily everyone. It usually is experienced with intense fear, terror, and helplessness (subjective dimension of stressor definition). Chronic illness, ordinary bereavement, marital discord, and business reverses are not considered sufficiently stressful to cause PTSD. DSM-III-R distinguishes stressors based on duration: predominantly acute events (duration of less than 6 months) and predominantly enduring circumstances (duration of greater than 6 months). Claimants in the vast majority of cases seen in civil litigation experience the stressor for only a few seconds.

The stressor criteria for PTSD in DSM-IV are slightly but significantly different. The normative aspects of the DSM-III-R definition, such as "a psychologically distressing event that is outside the range of usual human experience" (American Psychiatric Association 1987, p. 247) and "the stressor producing this syndrome would be markedly distressing to almost anyone" (p. 247), have been deleted from DSM-IV. Thus, the stressor criteria definition has been broadened. DSM-IV also dropped the distinction between stressors of acute and enduring duration. As a consequence, individuals with extreme reactions to minor trauma may pass through the wider gate of the DSM-IV traumatic stressor criteria (Pilowsky 1992).

The traumatic stressors as defined by DSM-III-R and DSM-IV that are most commonly associated with PTSD include serious threats to the life or bodily integrity of the person, his or her spouse, children, close relatives, or friends (American Psychiatric Association 1987, pp. 247–248; 1994, p. 424). Sudden destruction of a person's home or community and witnessing the injury or death of another through accident or violence constitute traumatic stressors frequently associated with the development of PTSD. Stressors caused by man appear to have a greater traumatic impact than natural events. The injured person usually feels that a man-made stressor is preventable, whereas natural disasters are unavoidable acts of God. Feelings of rage, retribution, and vengeance are commonly experienced. Litigation, which is a frequent development, further exposes the person to psychological trauma inflicted by the legal system. Torture frequently will produce severe PTSD symptoms. By contrast, commonly occurring car accidents without significant physical injury are less likely to produce PTSD symptomatology. McFarlane (1988) reported that the best clinical predictor of later PTSD development was an initial disturbance in concentration and memory. In a study (Koopman et al. 1994) of the survivors of the 1991 Oakland/Berkeley firestorm, dissociative symptoms strongly predicted posttraumatic stress symptoms measured 7–9 months after the firestorm.

On the other hand, data from DSM-IV field trials indicate that the clinical constellation of PTSD symptoms remains relatively constant across a spectrum of traumatic stressor definitions (Green 1992). Thus the stressor criterion does not appear to be as critical as originally thought. In the forensic context, however, the use of broadly framed definitional criteria for the traumatic stressor raises concerns about the abuse of the PTSD diagnosis in litigation, particularly since PTSD symptom evaluation relies almost entirely on the subjective reporting of the litigant.

Breslau et al. (1991) compared the prevalence of PTSD by type of event. They found that sudden injury or a serious accident was associated with a lower rate of PTSD (11.6%) than was physical assault (22.6%). In fact, the rate of PTSD varied only a little over a spectrum of events such as seeing someone killed or seriously hurt (23.6%), news of sudden death or accident of a close relative or friend (21.1%), or threat to life (24.0%). Only women who reported rape had a significantly higher rate of PTSD (80%). The most brutalized prisoners of war experienced a lifetime PTSD prevalence of greater than 90% (Sutker et al. 1991). With the exception of rape, less than 25% of those exposed to typical PTSD stressors developed this disorder. Within the population studied, the majority of men acquired PTSD through combat experience or civilian physical attack. Most women developed PTSD symptoms following sexual assault or victimization through crime. Helzer et al. (1987) reported a lifetime PTSD rate of 9.3% in Vietnam War combat veterans and 3% in persons who were mugged 18 months before being interviewed. The highest PTSD rate of 20% was found in the subgroup of wounded veterans. A lifetime prevalence for PTSD of 1.3% was found in a community survey in North Carolina, "placing it above panic disorder, bipolar disorder, and schizophrenia with respect to lifetime frequency in the population sampled" (Davidson et al. 1990b, p. 259). Symptoms of PTSD that do not meet the full criteria for the diagnosis of PTSD (subthreshold PTSD) are quite common.

Traumatic stress studies generally indicate that even devastating, extremely traumatic events usually do not lead to more than 50% of the exposed population developing PTSD (Green 1982; Lystad 1988). Thus examiners must not automatically assume that a PTSD qualifying stressor will necessarily produce PTSD. The presence of a PTSD qualifying stressor should lead the examiner to search for PTSD symptoms but not blindly conclude that PTSD must be present in the absence of qualifying criteria.

PTSD studies, however, may not accurately describe the typical person with PTSD. Most persons with PTSD do not seek professional help or come to research attention (Tomb 1994). Persons with PTSD avoid thinking or talking about their trauma and symptoms. Thus the subset found in research studies may not be typical of the majority.

Axis IV of both DSM-III-R and DSM-IV is used for reporting psychosocial and environmental problems that may influence diagnosis, treatment, and the prognosis of mental disorders. The traumatic stressor categories of Axis IV in DSM-III-R are defined in normative terms. That is, the severity rating of the stressor is based on the clinician's assessment of the stress that an "average" person under similar circumstances and with similar sociocultural values would experience from the particular stressor(s) occurring in the year preceding the current evaluation (American Psychiatric Association 1987, p. 19).

In DSM-IV, the normative criterion of the "average" person is eliminated. The requirement that the traumatic stressor must have occurred within a year prior to the evaluation is no longer hard and fast in DSM-IV. The exact DSM-IV language states that "the clinician may choose to note psychosocial and environmental problems occurring prior to the previous year if these clearly contribute to the mental disorder or have become a focus of treatment . . ." (American Psychiatric Association 1994, p. 29). The effect of liberalized language changes is to implicitly expand the subjective aspects of the definition of traumatic stressors. In DSM-IV, the person's psychological susceptibility to developing PTSD after exposure to a defined traumatic stressor is a valid consideration.

PTSD is the only exception to the requirement that the stressor must have occurred within a year prior to the evaluation. The stressor assessment focuses on the amount of change caused in the person's life, the degree to which the event is desired and under the person's control, and the number of stressors. The example is given in DSM-III-R of a planned pregnancy as usually being less stressful than an unwanted pregnancy. In DSM-III-R, the stressor assessment is based on the normative severity of the stressor, not the particular vulnerability of a person to certain stressors. On the DSM-III-R Severity of Psychological Stressors Scale: Adults, only stressors termed as extreme (code 5) or catastrophic (code 6) would likely qualify as sufficiently traumatic to produce PTSD (American Psychiatric Association 1987, p. 11). The numerical coding of stressors has been dropped from DSM-IV. Instead, clinicians are instructed to list relevant psychosocial and environmental problem categories specified in DSM-IV and indicate the specific factors involved.

The definition of the traumatic stressors in normative terms comes closest to a pure stressor model of PTSD. Defining the stressor criteria reasonably narrowly prevents trivializing the diagnosis of PTSD through unwarranted widespread use. DSM-III-R specifies that if vulnerability to stress exists, it frequently will be due to another mental disorder that should be coded on Axis I or II (American Psychiatric Association 1987, p. 19). Nevertheless, a stressor-susceptibility model of PTSD accords more credibly with clinical reality. No PTSD criteria for individual susceptibility to stress are present in DSM-IV. By removing the normative language, however, DSM-IV implicitly expands the subjective component in defining a traumatic stressor.

Clinical experience and the psychiatric literature do support the proposition that certain people, due to specific vulnerabilities, are more susceptible to the development of PTSD, including its chronic form. A study of twins clearly identified genetic susceptibility for the development of PTSD symptoms (True et al. 1993). Bremner et al. (1993a) found that patients who sought treatment for combat-related PTSD had higher rates of childhood physical abuse than combat veterans without PTSD. The existence of prior or concomitant psychiatric disorders adversely potentiates the internal perception of the danger posed by the traumatic event. Generally, clinicians take an interactional approach, assuming that neither personality characteristics nor aspects of the traumatic stressor alone determine outcome (Green et al. 1985a). Clinically, personality and the individual meaning of the stressor must be understood to properly assess and treat the patient (McFarlane 1990). Individual perception determines reality for the victim. Miller (G. H. Miller, personal communication, September 1992) distinguishes a stressor as an external event from trauma as an internal perception. In other words, stressor + individual susceptibility = trauma. He would rename PTSD as PSTD or poststress traumatic disorder. Stressor research has not clarified whether a minor stress, if experienced long enough, can produce sufficient traumatic stress to cause PTSD.

Risk factors for exposure to traumatic events have been identified. In one study (Breslau et al. 1991), male sex, less than a college education, extraversion, neuroticism, a history of three or more early conduct problems, and a family history of psychiatric disorder or substance abuse problems were shown to significantly increase the risk of exposure to traumatic events. Risk factors for the development of PTSD after exposure to traumatic stress included female sex, neuroticism, early separation, preexisting anxiety depression, family history of anxiety, and a family history of antisocial behavior (Breslau et al. 1991).

A number of factors affect the duration and severity of the response to the traumatic stressor, including the severity and duration of the stressor, genetic predisposition, developmental phase, age, prior traumatization, preexisting personality, and social support system (van der Kolk 1987). Litigation also may contribute adversely to the duration and severity of PTSD symptoms. In persons who developed PTSD that lasted longer than 1 year, the specific factors of a history of an antisocial family and female sex further identified this group (Breslau and Davis 1992). Comorbidity also appears to be associated with the development and maintenance of PTSD symptoms (Breslau and Davis 1992). The nature of the association is unclear. Hypotheses include the following: 1) the presence of comorbid conditions increase susceptibility and reactivity to traumatic stressors; 2) comorbid conditions are a complication of PTSD; and 3) comorbid conditions contribute to maintaining PTSD symptoms. Other predisposing vulnerability factors include locus of control (internal versus external), heavy alcohol or drug use, and recent life stresses.

The perception of less psychological support shortly after a trauma was predictive of PTSD on follow-up assessments, whereas more severe injury did not predict PTSD (Perry et al. 1992). Thus patients with less severe injuries and less psychological support were more likely to meet criteria for PTSD. Empirically, clinicians have known that psychological support mitigates the severity of psychological responses to traumatic stress. For example, experience with Vietnam War veterans and rape victims clearly shows that the presence of a support system markedly improves the clinical prognosis for these people. Raifman (1983) points out that one of the qualifying factors in determining whether a traumatic stressor is "outside the range of common experience" is the absence in society of organized rituals or support systems to help the traumatized person to cope with his or her experience.

Overwhelming trauma damages basic trust in ourselves and in the world. Thus individuals who already are impaired in basic trust are particularly vulnerable to this damaging trauma effect. Exposure to life-threatening trauma damages basic life assumptions, such as the world is a predictable and rational place, that bad things do not happen to good people, that persons in the position of authority will act responsibly, and that we are in control of our lives. Without some level of belief in these assumptions, we could not leave home or cross a street.

In the law, the issue of a litigant's vulnerability in personal injury cases usually is considered under the heuristic construct of the so-called *eggshell skull* or *eggshell psyche* plaintiff (Keeton et al. 1984; *Salley v. Childs* 1988; *Gammons v. Osteopathic Hospital of Maine, Inc.* 1987). An eggshell plaintiff is a person who is extremely vulnerable to even a minor trauma but has remained asymptomatic prior to the injury. The actor who cracks a plaintiff's eggshell skull, even if the trauma is minimal, is legally responsible for the damages that ensue. He or she cannot complain that the injured person was not a perfect specimen (Kionka 1977). On the other hand, in *Theriaulta v. Swan* (1989), the Supreme Judicial Court of Maine distinguished between an ordinarily sensitive person and a supersensitive plaintiff:

> In order to recover for either negligent or reckless infliction of emotional distress, a plaintiff must demonstrate that the harm alleged reasonably could have been expected to befall the ordinarily sensitive person [citations omitted]. When the harm reasonably could affect only the hurt feelings of the supersensitive plaintiff—the eggshell psyche—there is no entitlement to recovery. If however, the harm reasonably could have been expected to befall the ordinarily sensitive person, the tortfeasor must take his victim as he finds her, extraordinarily sensitive or not.

Using the eggshell skull hypothesis solely as a metaphor for the generically vulnerable plaintiff blurs the important distinction between a preexisting asymptomatic state and a symptomatic state. Mental functioning is a dynamic process, not a static structure like a skull. For example, the psychological resistance to trauma may vary over a 24-hour cycle. In forensic practice, it is rare to find a person alleging psychological injuries who has not had some prior relevant psychological symptoms, especially triggered by fatigue, physical illness, or other stress factors. Thus the legal concept of the eggshell plaintiff, although essential to the deliberations of the law, appears to be a distinct exception in forensic practice.

Claimants who do not have a prior history of psychiatric disorders often experience an acute, circumscribed PTSD without significant functional impairment, appearing to have a normal response to an abnormal stressor. Some experts view PTSD symptoms, in the main, as normal trauma-related reactions from which the vast majority of people improve without treatment (Cohen 1992). The problem arises, however, in distinguishing who will or will not ultimately develop persistent, pathological posttrauma symptoms. Blank (1993) observes that posttraumatic stress symptoms not adding up to PTSD are quite common and may represent normal responses to catastrophic situations that should be identified in the diagnostic nomenclature as a V code (conditions not attributable to a mental disorder). On the other hand, the vast majority of claimants with prolonged, debilitating PTSD have a psychopathological response to a similar traumatic stressor that appears to be driven largely by preexisting psychiatric impairments.

Applied to PTSD, however, the concept of individual susceptibility conflicts with the established DSM-III-R normative gatekeeper definition of the traumatic stressor. Although PTSD is incident specific, the forensic examiner obviously must consider the existence of comorbid conditions and diagnose them if they are present. Persons who react to a minor stressor with PTSD symptoms are distinctly rare. In such cases, other causes of the PTSD should be suspected and investigated. Usually in these cases, the symptom response is not diagnosable as PTSD but as another Axis I or Axis II disorder. Under DSM-IV, the subjective component of the definition of a traumatic stressor implicitly takes into account individual susceptibility.

The development of PTSD following low-magnitude stressors, however, is reported in the professional literature. Burstein (1985) reported that 8 of 73 PTSD cases developed following a low-magnitude or usual event, such as marital disruption, illegal acts, arrests of teenage children, failed adoption plans, and death of a loved one. Helzer et al. (1987) found that events cited by women that precipitated PTSD included a spouse's affair, a poisoning, and a miscarriage. These studies did not attempt to specifically rule out reactivated PTSD symptoms from previous traumas or from other current sources. *Cryptotrauma* and an *invisible trauma* have been described that may purportedly lead to PTSD (Scrignar 1988, pp. 63–79). Cryptotrauma does not produce PTSD. Rather, the forensic examiner does not appreciate the full impact of the traumatic stressor on the litigant. With invisible trauma, the traumatic stressor cannot be perceived by the senses (e.g., toxic substances) but nevertheless purportedly produces stress through the knowledge of its presence.

In tort cases involving toxicity, litigants may claim that they develop PTSD upon learning that they have been unwittingly exposed to toxic substances over the years or during some period of time in the past. Hindsight traumatization of prior personal exposure to originally nontraumatic events, however, does not accord conceptually with PTSD stressor criteria. The traumatic stressor either produces or fails to produce PTSD *at the time the stressor is experienced,* even in delayed PTSD. When a person experiences stress by discovering frightening information that permits previous non-traumatic events to be viewed as traumatic, the stressor ordinarily is not of sufficient strength to produce PTSD. However, another psychiatric disorder may develop. If PTSD does develop, the symptom content should reflect the stressful events surrounding being informed of the danger.

Pseudo-PTSD may arise in tort litigation involving toxicity. A reasonable fear of increased risk of cancer or other diseases after a toxic incident may be erroneously diagnosed as PTSD. The stressor necessary to produce PTSD is defined in DSM-III-R and DSM-IV as acutely life threatening, producing terror, intense fear, helplessness, and horror. Combined with the ubiquity of toxic agents ever present in our environment, the psychological stress related to a toxic event may not rise to an immediate life-threatening status. Perr (1993), in a review of 48 cases of claims of psychic injury due to exposure to asbestos, found that 19% alleged PTSD as a basis for damages. Perr concluded that the application of the PTSD concept to chronic illness was inappropriate because it does not meet the symptoms or stressor criteria for PTSD. If, on the other hand, toxic exposure occurs in association with an explosion or other life-threatening event, then the likelihood increases that the exposed person may develop PTSD.

In *Sterling v. Velsicol Chemical Corp* (1988), the Sixth Circuit Court of Appeals concluded that the alleged causes of PTSD must be closely scrutinized:

> Plaintiffs' drinking or otherwise using contaminated water, even over an extended period of time, does not constitute the type of recognizable stressor identified either by professional medical organizations or courts. Examples of stressors upon which courts have based awards for PTSD include rape, assault, military combat, fires, floods, earthquakes, car and airplane crashes, torture, and even internment in concentration camps, each of which are natural or man-made disasters with immediate or extended violent consequences. Whereas consumption of contaminated water may be an unnerving occurrence, it does not rise to the level of the type of psychologically traumatic event that is a universal stressor. A plaintiff's claim that a particular event or series of events caused him PTSD must be subjected to the closest scrutiny. The court must demand that a plaintiff produce sufficient authority that the particular event con-

stitutes a "recognized stressor" or a psychologically traumatic event which would produce significant symptoms of distress in almost everyone experiencing such an event. In the instant case, the plaintiffs produced none, and this court can identify no relevant authority that the consumption of contaminated water is a recognized stressor upon which an award of PTSD can rest. Additionally, plaintiff's experts presented no evidence establishing that any of the plaintiffs were, in fact, "retraumatized" through recurrent and intrusive recollections or dreams of drinking the contaminated water. Plaintiff Johnson's nightmares about "what was happening to [his] children and [constant preoccupation] with what their condition was and . . . might be in the future" merely describe his reasonable fear of increased risk of cancer and other disease. Since each plaintiff failed to satisfy all of the criteria necessary for a diagnosis of PTSD, we reverse the district court's award of damages.

Arguing backwards from the claimant's PTSD to specific causes or events as a defense in criminal cases or as a basis for a claim for damages in tort cases is problematic. Courts have given a mixed reception to inferring from the diagnosis of PTSD that an alleged traumatic event occurred. Thus in *State v. Kim* (1982), a child psychiatrist was permitted to testify concerning rape trauma syndrome to establish that rape had occurred by a family member. The expert said that the complainant child's symptoms were "consistent with" symptoms in his other cases of child rape by a family member. On the other hand, in *Spencer v. General Electric Company* (1988), the court rejected the admission of a PTSD diagnosis to establish the disorder's triggering event, in this case that an alleged prior rape had occurred. The court noted the division of authority regarding the admission of PTSD testimony: "PTSD is simply a diagnostic category created by psychiatrists . . . to help identify, predict and treat emotional problems experienced by the counselors, clients or patients. It was not developed or devised as a tool for ferreting out the truth in cases where it is hotly disputed whether the rape occurred." The presence of PTSD symptoms presumes, by definition, an antecedent traumatic stressor. Clinically, this presumption is accepted as a matter of course. In the context of litigation, however, courts may find that it lacks probative value.

The following clinical vignette illustrates the problems that arise concerning the sufficiency of traumatic stressors:

> A 29-year-old, married minister is involved in a very minor traffic accident. His car is struck from behind at approximately 4 mph, producing a loud bang but only superficially denting his bumper and breaking the left rear

taillight. After the accident, recurrent dreams and flashbacks begin and are prominent symptoms. His treating physician makes the diagnosis of PTSD. A lawsuit is filed against the defendant on the grounds of negligence causing psychological injury.

The claimant is examined by a forensic psychiatrist who learns that the minister's father committed suicide 9 months prior to the accident. Moreover, his father, who was intoxicated at the time, placed a gun in his mouth and shot himself in front of his son. Past history reveals that the son experienced severe child abuse at the hands of his father.

Shortly after the auto accident, the minister becomes preoccupied with the collision. He particularly is bothered by auditory flashbacks of the gun being fired. He begins to gradually experience, for the first time, recurrent dreams containing vivid visual images of expanding pumpkin heads and gory scenes. Before his father's death, the claimant was prudent in his actions and morally scrupulous. After the father's suicide, he neglected his duties, spent money frivolously, had an affair, and began to gamble. He complains that he experiences feelings of detachment from others, guilty thoughts that he failed to save his father, and feelings that his life will be over soon. He has lost 15 lbs. and has trouble falling asleep. Formerly of placid temperament, he flies into rages at parishioners. Proceedings were underway before the accident to relieve the claimant of his position as minister and to try to persuade him to seek professional help.

The forensic psychiatrist makes the diagnosis of delayed PTSD but relates it to witnessing his father's suicide rather than the car accident. It also is determined that the claimant was disabled for his work as a minister well before the car accident by typical prodromal symptoms of PTSD.

This vignette illustrates the critical importance of thoroughly investigating the traumatic stressor. Minor stressors that allegedly cause PTSD must be met with commonsense skepticism. In this case, the court will determine whether the minor car accident was the "final straw" that triggered the full blown PTSD or find that the PTSD would have emerged anyway.

As part of a credible forensic examination, other stressors in the claimant's life need to be considered. Most of us live in a world of multiple stressors. The forensic examiner must not be deterred by the claimant's assertions concerning the cause of psychological impairments. Comorbid disorders associated with *multiple* psychological stressors may contribute significantly to the clinical picture (Breslau et al. 1991).

For PTSD claimants, a thorough exploration of Axis IV psychosocial and environmental problems in DSM-IV must be conducted to rule in or out superseding, intervening traumatic events that break the chain of causation between the alleged traumatic stressor and the development of

PTSD symptoms (Keeton et al. 1984). The proximate cause of the PTSD symptoms may be another traumatic event that occurred either before the incident in question took place or before the emergence of the PTSD symptoms allegedly caused by the incident in question.

Proposed Guideline

In assessing the sufficiency of traumatic stressors for the diagnosis of PTSD, the forensic examiner should be guided by official diagnostic manuals, the professional literature, and current research. The possible contributions of multiple stressors to the PTSD claimant's clinical picture should be evaluated.

Preexisting Psychiatric History

It seems unnecessary to assert that a claimant's psychiatric history must be explored. Yet it is truly remarkable to observe how often psychiatric and psychological evaluations of PTSD claimants (as well as others) do not proceed beyond the claimant's allegations. It is as if the claimant's life began at the time of the alleged traumatic event. Once having entered the legal arena, some mental health professionals abandon their clinical positions and hard-won skills. No forensic psychiatric examination is credible without a thorough investigation of the claimant's past. Accordingly, attempts to restrict or constrain development of detailed historical information by either party to a litigation must be vigorously resisted.

In the evaluation of the PTSD claimant, the prior existence of PTSD must be considered. In a recent study, the lifetime prevalence of PTSD was found to be 9.2% (Breslau et al. 1991). Thus a preexisting base rate for PTSD exists in the population from which the PTSD claimant emerges. Moreover, as noted in the previous section, certain risk factors increase a person's exposure to traumatic events. Other risk factors increase the vulnerability to developing PTSD once exposure to traumatic events occurs. These risk factors usually are diagnosable as part of other Axis I and Axis II psychiatric disorders.

An observable deficiency in a number of forensic evaluations is the absent assessment of Axis II personality disorders that may be clearly germane to the claimant's current clinical picture. Also traumatic stressors may not produce PTSD but may instead exacerbate or reactivate preexisting Axis I and II psychiatric disorders or contribute to the development of a new mental disorder. To complicate matters further, PTSD has been reported to mimic personality disorders (Van Putten and Emory 1973; Walker 1981). Consistent with the increased awareness of comorbid conditions by clinicians, Green et al. (1985c) found that antisocial personality disorder and alcohol and drug dependence were diagnoses consistently associated with PTSD. Others have observed the coexistence of PTSD with antisocial, borderline, and mixed personality disorders (Embry 1990).

There are 10 personality disorder diagnoses in DSM-IV. An 11th diagnosis, personality disorder not otherwise specified, is a category for disorders of personality functioning that are not classifiable as a specific personality disorder. One of the most common personality disorder diagnoses seen in litigation (and for that matter in clinical practice) is borderline personality disorder (BPD). The incidence of physical and sexual abuse in persons diagnosed with BPD is 67%–86% (Herman and van der Kolk 1987). In dissociative identity disorder (formerly called multiple personality disorder) (Axis I diagnosis), 98% of these patients report histories of severe childhood abuse beginning before the age of 5 (Bryer et al. 1987; Briere and Zaida 1989; Lowenstein 1991b). On careful questioning, 50%–60% of psychiatric inpatients, 40%–60% of psychiatric outpatients, and 70% of psychiatric emergency room patients report childhood histories of physical or sexual abuse or both (Herman 1992). Many of them developed PTSD as children as a consequence of their abuse (Eth and Pynoos 1985). In survivors of prolonged, repeated trauma a spectrum of conditions is produced, rather than a single disorder, that Herman (1992) proposes to call *complex posttraumatic stress disorder.*

The consistent reports of high rates of childhood trauma in borderline patients suggest that BPD may be a posttraumatic disorder (Ross 1991). On the other hand, Gunderson and Sabo (1993) conclude that borderline psychopathology develops from a history of abusive experiences that join other factors that shape enduring aspects of character. They assert that BPD and PTSD are clinically distinguishable disorders that often occur together and have certain overlapping symptoms. BPD is considered to be a vulnerability factor for the development of PTSD. In her studies of the Chowchilla school bus kidnapping, Terr (1983) noted that the aftermath of the psychic trauma caused by the incident produced permanent personality changes in the children. The presence of early trauma tends to produce a symptom complex that includes self abuse, dissociative phenomena, chronic mood, and personality changes rather than the classic PTSD symptoms of adults. The coexistence of PTSD with personality disorders is noted in the psychiatric literature (Southwick et al. 1993a).

Because of the unfortunately high incidence of childhood physical and sexual abuse, forensic examiners should consider the presence of childhood PTSD as a precursor to any personality disorder, not just BPD, and assess its contribution to the claimant's current clinical presentation. Moreover, some claimants with alleged PTSD who appear to have functioned well prior to exposure to a traumatic event experience reactivation of nightmares and flashbacks of childhood abuse. A consequent deterioration in their functioning ensues. The commingling of current PTSD symptoms and resurrected traumatic memories from the past can present an extremely complicated clinical picture. Trying to separate past from present symptomatology can be a forensic evaluation nightmare. The developmental psychopathology of children and adolescents exposed to traumatic stress is described by Pynoos (1993).

Preexisting medical disorders and drug treatment for both psychiatric and physical disorders (especially associated with physical injury and pain) may complicate or worsen the claimant's clinical picture. Breslau et al. (1991) found in their sample of 1,007 young adults that a high incidence of other psychiatric disorders coexisted with PTSD. The adjusted odds ratio that another psychiatric disorder coexisted in persons with PTSD versus those with no PTSD is shown in Table 3–7.

Table 3–7. Adjusted odds ratio that another psychiatric disorder coexisted in persons with PTSD versus those with no PTSD

Disorder	Adjusted odds ratio[a]
Obsessive-compulsive disorder	10.28
Agoraphobia	6.42
Dysthymia	6.11
Mania	6.05
Panic	5.70
Major depression	4.39
Generalized anxiety disorder	2.75
Drug abuse and dependence	2.75
Alcohol abuse or dependence	2.23
Any substance abuse or dependence	2.86
Any disorder	6.30

[a]Odds ratio adjusted for sex.
Source. Adapted from Breslau et al. 1991.

In another study, it was found that cocaine-opiate users are over three times as likely as comparison subjects to report a traumatic event and to report more symptoms and events, and are more likely to meet diagnostic criteria for PTSD (Cottler et al. 1992). Antidepressant, antipsychotic, anti-anxiety, and sleep medications can produce anxiety, depression, and nightmares. Pain medications are notorious for the exacerbation or induction of a depressive disorder. In DSM-III-R and DSM-IV, Axis III is used to indicate any current physical disorder or condition that is relevant to the understanding or management of a case.

With the odds so high that another psychiatric disorder may coexist with PTSD, the forensic psychiatrist clearly must attempt to rule out other conditions when a diagnosis of PTSD is made. The high likelihood that other Axis I, II, and III disorders and conditions coexist makes it difficult to identify pure PTSD cases. This fact has confounded and limited biological research into PTSD. No forensic evaluation can be credible without a thorough examination of the claimant's psychiatric history.

The following clinical vignette shows a complex psychiatric history and its impact on the assessment of the current clinical picture of the claimant:

> A 23-year-old, single secretary is electrically shocked when she touches a copying machine. The electrical jolt causes her to drop her papers. Immediately thereafter, she is unable to work. She cannot leave the house in the morning because she is afraid to turn on the toaster, throw light switches, or use her hair dryer. She cannot drive her car because she is afraid to switch on the ignition. The claimant is evaluated by a forensic examiner who makes the initial diagnosis of PTSD but does not evaluate her past history. The claimant remembers her traumatic event frequently, but she does not display any intrusive, unbidden thoughts or memories associated with intense feelings. Recurrent nightmares depicting sadistic abuse of children are reported by the claimant. These dreams also occurred before the traumatic event.
>
> When additional medical records become available, the forensic examiner realizes that the claimant has a significant psychiatric history. She decides to see the claimant again and inquire further into the claimant's past. The claimant was hospitalized twice for major depression at ages 17 and 20. In the hospital records, a concurrent Axis II BPD was diagnosed. Work records reveal sporadic employment with poor peer relationships. School records show frequent absences. It is stated in the school records that the patient frequently stayed home by herself. A psychiatrist's note to the school describes mood instability and social withdrawal. Moreover, the claimant's mother died 2 months prior to the accident. The mother had

been physically and sexually abusive to the claimant between ages 3 and 9. Her recurrent nightmares of children being abused relates to the claimant's childhood abuse. The electrical shock became the "straw" that resurfaced a number of early abuse experiences involving being tied up and beaten with an electrical cord.

The forensic examiner revises her diagnosis to simple phobia, due to the claimant's almost total avoidance of any electrical devices and the absence of PTSD symptoms. An Axis II diagnosis of BPD (exacerbated) is made along with the diagnoses of PTSD from childhood manifesting now primarily through her recurrent nightmares of her child abuse and BPD. The defendants in this case are responsible for the simple phobia and the exacerbation of the BPD but not the childhood PTSD. Diagnostic clarification by the forensic examiner allows for reasonable allocation of damages, treatment recommendations such as referral of the claimant to a phobia clinic, and an appropriate period of psychotherapy (Nally and Saigh 1993).

Proposed Guideline

A credible forensic psychiatric evaluation of a PTSD claimant requires a thorough examination of the claimant's psychiatric and medical history, including review of prior medical, psychiatric, and other pertinent records.

Subjective Reporting of PTSD

With the possible exception of behavioral reenactments of the traumatic events, no objective clinical signs and symptoms exist for PTSD. Thus the forensic examiner must not rely solely on the subjective reporting of the claimant. Additional sources of information must be obtained. The possibility of malingered PTSD in the litigation context must always be considered. In PTSD, the trauma becomes the central issue in the patient's life. Life is structured around avoiding stimuli that cause psychophysiologic arousal (fear and terror). Collateral sources of information can help confirm or deny this life centrality aspect of PTSD. The subjective nature of PTSD symptoms, as with many other psychiatric disorders, presents special problems in litigation.

Psychophysiologic studies hold out the promise of providing more objective data in the evaluation of PTSD symptoms (Bremner et al. 1993c;

Charney et al. 1993; Southwick et al. 1993b) (see also Chapter 5, this volume). Short-term and long-term neurobiological consequences of severe, overwhelming stress have been identified by psychobiologic research. In the forensic context, Pitman and Orr (1993) found that the differences in physiologic responses to "imaginal stimuli" between persons suffering from PTSD and control subjects varied significantly. Measurements of heart rate, sweat gland activity, and facial muscle tension were significantly higher in PTSD patients.

Laboratory testing may have an important impact in PTSD litigation where its presence or absence is at issue. Although psychophysiological testing of PTSD brought into court may be skeptically looked upon as a magical "black box" of forensic psychiatrists, it may prove very useful as an adjunct to more traditional methods of psychiatric evaluation. Informed clinical knowledge, judgment, and experience remain the best tools for the diagnosis of PTSD. For example, the natural progression of emotional reactions following trauma typically move from anxiety to depression or to a combination of anxiety and depression. Embellishers usually reverse the sequence or emphasize anxiety or depression to the exclusion of the other. Issues of admissibility of such evidence in civil and criminal litigation remain. So far, only one court has allowed graphs of the plaintiff's psychophysiologic responses to be presented to the jury as evidence that the psychophysiologic reactivity criteria for PTSD were met. No court has allowed psychophysiologic results to establish the diagnosis of PTSD (Pitman et al. 1994). If psychophysiologic testing of PTSD is viewed similarly to the methods of the polygrapher, such evidence may not be held to be admissible.

Psychiatrists who venture into the legal arena must be aware of the fundamentally different roles that exist between a treating psychiatrist and the forensic psychiatric expert (Simon 1994a). Treatment and expert roles do not mix. For example, unlike the orthopedist who possesses objective data such as an X ray of a broken limb to demonstrate orthopedic damages in court, the treating psychiatrist turned expert relies heavily on the subjective reporting of the patient. In the treatment context, psychiatrists are interested primarily in the patient's perception of his or her difficulties, not necessarily the objective reality. The DSM, for example, encourages clinicians to make diagnoses based on the self-reports of patients regardless of their accuracy. As a consequence, many treating psychiatrists do not speak to third parties or check pertinent records to gain additional information about a patient or to corroborate their statements. The law, however, is interested only in that which can reasonably be established by facts. Uncorroborated, subjective patient data are frequently attacked in court as being speculative, self-serving, and unreliable. The treating psychiatrist cannot effectively counter these charges.

Credibility issues also abound. The treating psychiatrist is, and must be, an ally of the patient. This bias toward the patient is a proper treatment stance that fosters the therapeutic alliance. Furthermore, for the psychiatrist to effectively treat the psychiatric patient, the patient needs to be "liked" by the psychiatrist. No practitioner can treat a patient for very long who is fundamentally disliked. Moreover, the psychiatrist looks for mental disorders to treat. This again is an appropriate bias for the treating psychiatrist.

In court, credibility is a critical commodity to possess when testifying. Opposing counsel will take every opportunity to portray the treating psychiatrist as a subjective mouthpiece for the patient-litigant—which may or may not be true. Also, court testimony by the treating psychiatrist may compel the disclosure of information that may not be *legally* privileged but nonetheless is viewed as intimate and confidential by the patient. This disclosure in court by the previously trusted therapist is bound to cause psychological damage to the therapeutic relationship (Strasburger 1987). In addition, psychiatrists must be careful to inform patients about the consequences of releasing treatment information, particularly in legal matters. Section 4, Annotation 2 of the *Principles of Medical Ethics: With Annotations Especially Applicable to Psychiatry* (Ethics Committee of the American Psychiatric Association 1992) states,

> The continuing duty of the psychiatrist to protect the patient includes fully apprising him/her of the connotations of waiving the privilege of privacy. This may become an issue when the patient is being investigated by a government agency, is applying for a position, or is involved in legal action. (p. 6)

Finally, when the treating psychiatrist testifies concerning the need for further treatment, a conflict of interest is readily apparent. In making such treatment prognostications, the psychiatrist stands to benefit economically from his or her recommendation of further treatment. Although this may not be the intention of the psychiatrist at all, opposing counsel is sure to point out that the psychiatrist has a financial interest in the case.

In its ethics statement, the American Academy of Psychiatry and the Law advises that "a treating psychiatrist should generally avoid agreeing to be an expert witness or to perform an evaluation of his patient for legal purposes because a forensic evaluation usually requires that other people be interviewed and testimony may adversely affect the therapeutic relationship" (American Academy of Psychiatry and the Law 1991).

The treating psychiatrist should attempt to remain solely in a treatment role (Simon 1992b). If it becomes necessary to testify on behalf of the patient, the treating psychiatrist should testify only as a fact witness rather than as an expert witness. As a fact witness, the psychiatrist will be asked to describe the number and length of visits, diagnoses, and treatment. Generally, no opinion evidence will be requested concerning causation of the injury or the extent of damages. In some jurisdictions, however, the court may convert a fact witness into an expert at the time of trial. Psychiatrists must remain ever mindful of the many double-agent roles that can develop when mixing psychiatry and litigation (Simon 1992a).

The forensic expert, on the other hand, is usually free from these encumbrances. No doctor-patient relationship is created during forensic evaluation with its attendant treatment biases toward the patient. The expert can review a variety of records and can speak to a number of people who know the litigant. Furthermore, the forensic expert is not as easily distracted from considering exaggeration or malingering because of a clear appreciation of the litigation context and the absence of treatment bias (Simon 1994b). Finally, the forensic expert is not placed in a conflict-of-interest position of recommending treatment from which he or she would personally benefit. The forensic expert, however, is frequently viewed by opposing counsel as a biased "hired gun."

The following clinical vignette illustrates the different roles of the treating psychiatrist and forensic examiner in the evaluation of the subjective reporting of PTSD symptoms:

> A 41-year-old transit worker states that he witnessed a subway collision in which a number of passengers were killed. Thereafter, he was unable to work. He is seen in brief psychotherapy. Because of "classic" PTSD symptoms, the clinician does not hesitate to make the diagnosis of PTSD. The diagnosis is duly recorded in the treatment record. Three months after the accident, the claimant reports recurrent nightmares that replay the traumatic event in faithful detail. The claimant also mentions that he is avoiding friends and social events.
>
> Examination by a forensic examiner reveals a history of juvenile delinquency. Classic textbook PTSD symptoms are reported by the claimant. Military records indicate that the claimant was dishonorably discharged after serving time in the brig for breaking and entering. A military psychiatrist diagnosed antisocial personality. Moreover, witnesses place the

claimant at 1,000 feet from the crash site where a curve in the tunnel obstructs the view of the crash. Video surveillance evidence shows that the claimant is dating, playing basketball, and going away on weekend excursions. The forensic examiner makes the diagnosis of malingering.

An obvious problem for the treating psychiatrist was the total lack of suspicion concerning malingering. This is not unusual in the treatment context because the treating psychiatrist assumes the patient has come for help rather than to build his or her own legal case. It is assumed that the person has a wellness agenda, not a legal agenda. In the litigation context, however, the possibility of malingering always must be considered. For example, in 1980, the Veterans Administration announced that "PTSD delayed type" was a compensable disorder. Psychiatric examiners were inundated by claimants who presented with a symptom checklist that had been published previously (Goodwin and Guze 1984). Some claimants who were never in Vietnam gave elaborate stories of combat (Kinzie 1989).

Proposed Guideline

Relying solely on the subjective reporting of symptoms by the PTSD claimant without considering additional sources of information is insufficient. As a corollary, treater and forensic roles should not be mixed in the forensic examination of the PTSD claimant.

Assessing Functional Impairment

Mental disability, depending on the circumstances, can be a legal basis for compensation (Spaulding 1991). In personal injury cases, the PTSD claimant seeks monetary damages for psychic injury and consequent impairment inflicted by the alleged negligence of another party. The forensic examiner must be able to conduct a competent assessment of the presence or absence of a litigant's functional impairment. In DSM-IV, the diagnosis of PTSD contains an additional criteria for "clinically significant distress or impairment in social, occupational, or other important areas of functioning" (American Psychiatric Association 1994, p. 429).

The forensic examiner is presented with a number of unique problems when conducting the psychiatric or psychological examination of the claimant. Because of the adversarial context and the stated lack of confidentiality of forensic examinations, a self-disclosure by the claimant is generally inhibited. Scheduling of the examination is another issue. Some experts recommend conducting the entire interview at one sitting, thus allowing the examiner to assess the claimant's ability to function in a worklike situation (Enelow 1991). With PTSD claimants, however, it may be necessary to have several time-limited interviews. Discussing the litigant's traumatic experience may evoke intense symptoms that can be managed more comfortably over the course of shorter interviews. Further, marathon interviews tend to be fatiguing and counterproductive for both the claimant and examiner. Lengthy interviews may be viewed by the claimant as harassing.

Psychological testing can be an important adjunct to a comprehensive forensic examination. By contrast, the use of self-report instruments provides a structural protocol for obtaining the patient's complaints. Self-report instruments are not psychological tests, however, nor are the data collected scientifically defensible as anything other than the subjective reporting of the litigant (Enelow 1991). Grossly inaccurate or biased courtroom testimony by psychiatric expert witnesses may be related, in part, to the widespread use of shortcut diagnoses by checklists that have largely replaced descriptive psychiatry (Sparr and Boehnlein 1990). Even the use of standardized measures of psychopathology such as the Brief Psychiatric Rating Scale (BPRS), the Standard Assessment of Depressive Disorders (SADD), and the Global Assessment Scale (GAS) as well as structured and semistructured interviews may have limited value because they were not developed for the litigation context.

Standardized psychological tests may provide additional important data, particularly when the claimant is unable to articulate his or her difficulties or appears to lack credibility. Psychological testing also can be valuable in detecting Axis II personality disorders that may be causing or contributing to the claimant's impairment. The forensic examiner may not be able to spend sufficient time with the claimant that usually is necessary for the diagnosis of personality disorders. The forensic examiner should have a working knowledge of the validity, reliability, and limitations of the psychological tests administered. It is the examiner's responsibility to integrate and explain the summary findings of psychological testing with data and conclusions from the psychiatric examination.

In conducting a forensic assessment of functional impairment, a few general concepts should be kept in mind. First, the presence of psychological symptoms do not necessarily equate with functional impairment. The examiner must find actual evidence of impairment through the claimant's psychiatric history, behavior, and the examination findings. Second, disability should be expressed quantitatively if the assessment method provides for a percentage or numerical evaluation. Third, the concept of convenient focus must be considered in every evaluation (Lasky 1991). The concept of convenient focus states that a preexisting disorder is uncovered by stress rather than created by it. Fourth, when an individual is not working, certain secondary effects occur. The various beneficial aspects of work are unavailable. Often, financial and marital difficulties ensue. The examiner must distinguish impairment that is a response to PTSD from the secondary consequences of not working.

Hirschfeld and Behan (Behan and Hirschfield 1963; Hirschfeld and Behan 1963; Hirschfeld and Behan 1966) proposed a paradigm of the injured worker that takes into account the personality difficulties and troubled life situation of the worker. In a number of cases, they found that an "accident" provided the occasion to assume a formerly unacceptable disabled role. The paradigm has been updated by Panzarella (1991) for psychological injury. Thus the claimant's tendency to ascribe all difficulties as stemming from beginning after a traumatic event or injury should not be initially accepted as factual.

DSM-III-R and DSM-IV use a comprehensive multiaxial evaluation system. The first three axes apply to official diagnostic assessments. Axis IV, as noted earlier, is used in assessing the severity of psychosocial stressors. Axis V, the Global Assessment of Functioning (GAF) Scale, provides a measure of an individual's psychological, social (including leisure activities), and occupational functioning. In DSM-IV, the numerical coding has been expanded from a scale of 0–90 to 0–100. Three additional proposed scales (Social and Occupational Functioning Assessment Scale [SOFA], Global Assessment of Relational Functioning [GARF], and the Defensive Styles Rating Scale) may be useful in special circumstances. Axis V reasonably measures adaptive functioning, though limited partly by its modest reliability (Goldman et al. 1992). As noted earlier, the current California workers' compensation system of rating psychological impairment requires the use of DSM-III-R diagnoses (Enelow 1991).

No matter how ominous a psychiatric diagnosis may appear on its face, courts rely on the claimant's *actual* level of functioning in assessing damages. For example, some chronic schizophrenic patients with long-standing hallucinations and delusions can take proper care of themselves and remain employable. A specific diagnosis, by itself, does not imply a given level of impairment.

For a complete assessment of functional impairment, Axis V of DSM-III-R or DSM-IV should be used with the American Medical Association's (AMA) *Guides to Evaluation of Permanent Impairment* (American Medical Association 1993). Other assessment approaches also are available (Panzarella 1991; *Guidelines for Handling Psychiatric Issues in Workers' Compensation Cases* 1988). It is not enough to rely on the forensic examiner's "clinical experience" in rendering impairment assessments of claimants. Such judgments can be idiosyncratic or even deviant when subject to litigation pressures.

The forensic examiner should use assessment methods that will provide a credible database for well-reasoned, defensible reports and opinions (Meyerson and Fine 1987). Forensic examiners must be prepared for vigorous cross-examination of their assessment methods (Babitsky and Sewall 1992). Accordingly, the forensic examiner should be knowledgeable in the use of the AMA Guides and be able to explain the general principles, their applicability, and the limitations in scientific validity and reliability. The latest edition of the AMA Guides should be used, unless otherwise specified by state statute in worker's compensation cases. Some states mandate use of specific editions. If the AMA Guides are not used, the forensic examiner's testimony may be found to lack probative value and be stricken (*Zebo v. Houston* 1990).

In assessing functional impairment, it would be extremely useful to know the natural, uncomplicated course of PTSD over time. Unfortunately, these data are very difficult to obtain because of the confounding factors in the nature and intensity of the stressor, the susceptibility of the person, and the presence or absence of a supportive environment. Green (1982), in reviewing the literature examining the psychological consequences of disaster, concluded that complex methodological problems prevent any accurate generalizations about the natural course of PTSD.

Nevertheless, a schematic chronology has been proposed by Horowitz (1983) of human psychological responses to stressful life events. An initial outcry is followed by phases of denial and intrusiveness leading to working through and completion. There is little definitive knowledge concerning the course of PTSD, however, as it relates to time of onset (Wolfe and Keane 1990). Scrignar (1988, pp. 87–95) asserts that PTSD, like all diseases or mental disorders, has an acute and chronic course. He divides PTSD into three stages: stage I—response to trauma; stage II—acute phase; and stage III—chronic phase. Scrignar lamented the deletion of chronic PTSD from DSM-III-R as unwarranted. Chronic PTSD has been reinstated in DSM-IV.

The determinants of acute, delayed onset and chronic PTSD have been examined by Robins et al. (1981). The acute PTSD group (duration of symptoms less than 6 months) had no major vulnerability factors or coexistent psychiatric disorder. The chronic PTSD group (duration of symptoms longer than 6 months) scored significantly higher on a number of vulnerability factors, including concurrent psychiatric disorder, family history of psychiatric disorder, avoidance personality traits, and being older. Blank (1993) finds ample evidence for acute, delayed, chronic, and intermittent or recurrent forms of PTSD regarding longitudinal course. Davidson et al. (1990a) studied the sequence of illness onset in PTSD in World War II and Vietnam War veterans.

In a rare prospective study of PTSD, Rothbaum et al. (1992) examined 95 female rape victims soon after assault. Subjects were assessed weekly for 12 weeks. Ninety-four percent of the women met PTSD criteria at the initial assessment, decreasing to 65% at assessment 4 and 47% at the final assessment (assessment 12). PTSD symptoms decreased sharply between assessments 1 and 4 for all women. Women whose PTSD persisted throughout the 3-month study did not show improvement after assessment 4. Women who did not meet PTSD criteria 3 months after the assault showed steady improvement over time. The study suggests that not all rape victims may require treatment because approximately one-half are expected to recover spontaneously. Rape victims with PTSD 2 months after assault appear unlikely to recover spontaneously. The responses and avoidance symptoms reported by all victims at 12 weeks after the assault indicates that anxiety symptoms may persist after PTSD symptoms improve or even remit.

Green et al. (1990a) reported a 12-year follow-up study of 120 survivors of the 1972 Buffalo Creek flood disaster in West Virginia. Between 1974 and 1986, the PTSD prevalence rate dropped from 44% to 28%. Symptom severity and levels of impairment declined significantly between 1974 and 1976. In general, most studies indicate that PTSD symptoms and impairment decline in severity over time (Hendin et al. 1984). Even if untreated, some PTSD claimant's symptoms will decrease over time, although a relapse is always possible. In the Breslau study (Breslau and Davis 1992), approximately 50% of the PTSD group studied had total remission of symptoms at 1 year following the traumatic event. This also was true for rape victims who had a PTSD development rate of 80% following trauma. At 3 years posttrauma, approximately one-third continued to manifest PTSD symptoms. In others, PTSD symptoms do not diminish but worsen in the absence of treatment or even with treatment. Hendin et al. (1984) found that 20% of a sample of 100 Vietnam War veterans with PTSD had chronic reexperiencing episodes. Kulka et al. (1990) found a PTSD prevalence rate of 15% in Vietnam War veterans in 1987–1988, approximately 19 years after exposure to war zone traumatic stress. Kluznik et al. (1986)

found a PTSD prevalence of 47% among World War II veterans 40 years after combat duty and confinement in prison camps.

It is rarely the situation that the forensic examiner has the unfettered opportunity to make a longitudinal assessment of impairment when conducting an examination of a claimant. Claimants are frequently on guard and suspicious of the examiner. This is an unavoidable artifact of the litigation context. The forensic examiner must obtain information from as many independent sources as possible to arrive at the claimant's pre- and postincident functioning.

Special considerations arise in the forensic psychiatric assessment of functional impairment, such as medications and situational effects. Frequently, claimants are taking medications. The effects of medications on various tasks used in assessing impairment must be considered. Medication may improve symptoms, but functional impairments may persist. Secondarily, the side effects of medication may produce significant impairment. For example, a number of psychotropic medications can induce both depression and side effects that are depressing.

What is the effect of the setting where the claimant is being assessed? Impairment assessments may be very difficult to conduct in noisy, distracting, or public settings, often leading to spurious results. Examinations conducted in the absence of privacy may compromise confidentiality and vitiate examination findings.

Generally, the presence of third parties distorts the interviewing process. Psychiatrists and other mental health professionals usually conduct patient interviews in a private atmosphere. In litigation, attorneys or their representatives may request to be present during the forensic evaluation. At a minimum, the presence of third parties is distracting to the intimate interactional process of interviewing. Other than with lovers, it is nowhere more apparent that three is a crowd.

When the attorney or his or her representative is present, the adversarial nature of the evaluation is heightened, even if the third party says nothing. Distrust becomes a major issue, making it very difficult for the forensic examiner to clinically engage the litigant and conduct an adequate examination. The experience becomes more like that of a deposition than a clinical interview. Under these stressful circumstances, the litigant may appear more psychologically regressed and symptomatic than usual, thus creating an artifact in the examination. On the other hand, if only family members are present, the litigant tends to feel more secure. Consequently, he or she may appear less clinically symptomatic and more functional than usual.

In some instances, it may be impossible to gain the claimant's cooperation unless he or she is initially accompanied into the interview by a family member (usually a spouse). Sometimes the claimant demands that a family member be present throughout the entire examination. Generally, however, the claimant becomes sufficiently comfortable with a non-confrontational examiner to relinquish the presence of the family member. Every effort should be made to see the claimant alone. If monitoring of the psychiatric interview must be done, unobtrusive audio or visual equipment can be used after the full knowledge and consent of all parties is obtained. As the examination progresses, both claimant and examiner gradually become less aware of the presence of monitoring equipment.

Rarely is a person totally impaired, either physically or mentally. The effects of rehabilitation and treatment are critical in determining permanent levels of impairment, if any. Assessments of permanent impairment usually must await the outcome of adequate rehabilitation and treatment.

Motivation for recovery is difficult to assess in the legal context. The claimant's concern about damaging the standing of his or her own legal case may inhibit motivation for improvement or recovery. In addition, with PTSD claimants, recounting the traumatic event in the course of litigation generally exacerbates PTSD symptomatology. Minimal impairment may lead to permanent disability when motivation for recovery is lacking. The level of motivation as a function of the mental disorder or of other factors is a critical determination.

Claimants are required to mitigate their damages (*Dohmann v. Richard* 1973). The meter cannot run forever against the defendant. Claimants with PTSD may resist obtaining psychiatric treatment because of a fear of worsening their symptoms by talking about the traumatic event. A variety of other reasons also may exist for not obtaining appropriate treatment, including concerns about jeopardizing the claimant's legal case. It is not unusual for the forensic examiner to be confronted by the anomalous situation of a significantly impaired claimant who has not obtained recommended treatment or who has been noncompliant with treatment recommendations. Numerous effective psychological and psychopharmacologic treatments are available for persons with PTSD (Kinzie 1989). Certain psychotropic drugs have been found to be effective against specific symptoms of PTSD (Davidson 1991; Sutherland and Davidson 1994). Fluoxetine was found to be effective in reducing reexperiencing, avoidance, and hyperarousal symptoms of PTSD (Nagy et al. 1993). Decreasing physiological arousal (fear and terror) is a core issue in treatment. The assessment of permanent impairment should not be attempted until the claimant has received a sufficient trial of appropriate treatment or the PTSD has sufficiently stabilized. An integrated treatment approach of PTSD has been proposed by Marmar et al. (1993).

The forensic examiner, in making long-term assessments of impairment, must distinguish between the PTSD claimant's continuing nonintrusive memory and reflection on a traumatic event versus dissociative reexperiencing phenomena. The PTSD claimant will always remember the traumatic event. As memory, the event can be important in molding a new adaptive world view. Moreover, the presence of actual PTSD symptoms years later may not necessarily cause impairment. Although approximately 30%–50% of natural disaster victims continue to manifest PTSD symptoms over time, the level of *functional* psychiatric impairment usually declines significantly (Green et al. 1990a; Green et al 1985b). Studies have demonstrated that PTSD is compatible with remarkable functional recovery (Goldstein et al. 1987; Roca et al. 1992). Blank (1993) noted that most studies of persons with PTSD have shown a degree of disjunction between the presence of the disorder and level of functioning. It is common to observe individuals with significant PTSD symptoms who function well.

On the other hand, severe PTSD is associated with significantly elevated risks for substance abuse, depression, anxiety disorders, self-destructive acts, family and other interpersonal disruption, and occupational impairment. Studies show that chronic combat-related PTSD frequently is associated with other psychiatric disorders. Coexisting phobias, major depression, and panic disorder may develop after the onset of the PTSD (Mellman et al. 1992). These disorders may be a reaction to PTSD symptoms rather than the original traumatic event. Again, the examiner must make a judgment call after careful assessment concerning the likelihood of chronic symptoms versus continuing improvement of PTSD symptoms.

It is reasonably well established, however, that persons with the persistent (chronic) form of PTSD likely will show a tendency toward deleterious personality change over time with severe functional incapacity (Reich 1990). McFarlane (1989), examining the predictors of chronic PTSD, found that the role of the trauma itself diminished over time and was eclipsed by premorbid variables such as neuroticism, prior adverse life events, and previous psychiatric disorder. On the other hand, Kulka et al. (1990) found that although personal characteristics played a significant role in chronicity, exposure to extreme events made a significant contribution to chronicity that was independent of background variables. Sutker et al. (1993) assessed current and long-term psychiatric sequelae of World War II Pacific Theater combat trauma in veterans and prisoners of war (POWs) 40 years later. Among the POW survivors, 70% met current criteria for PTSD and 78% for a lifetime diagnosis of PTSD. The combat veterans compared 18% and 29%, respectively.

In considering the PTSD claimant's prognosis and future treatment needs, the forensic examiner must weigh both impact event and personal factors in arriving at a final opinion. A number of posttrauma factors play a significant role in prognosis. For example, favorable factors include early treatment with sharing and validation of the victim's experience, early and continuing social support, exposure to therapeutic groups with other PTSD victims, avoidance of retraumatization, and avoidance of activities that interrupt or prevent treatment (e.g., lawsuits) (Tomb 1994). If possible, early reestablishment of a sense of community is essential when the latter has been damaged or lost.

The question concerning the effect of litigation on PTSD symptomatology and impairment has remained troublesome. Sales et al. (1984) found heightened symptoms among sexual assault victims at follow-up if their cases had been tried, compared with those who had not gone to trial. Unfortunately, the study does not clarify whether participation in litigation exacerbates symptoms or whether those with greater symptom severity sue. Green et al. (1990b), in a 14-year follow-up of survivors of the Buffalo Creek dam collapse of 1972, found no significant clinical differences between the litigant and nonlitigant survivor groups. On the other hand, Gleser et al. (1981) found clear relief among Buffalo Creek litigants after settlement as reflected in global test scores at 4 years postflood and 2 years postsettlement. One-third of subjects at early follow-up ascribed their improved mental functioning to a successful outcome or termination of litigation.

Clearly, involvement in the litigation process is a major psychological stressor. For the PTSD claimant, litigation continually stirs up painful memories or even flashbacks and nightmares of the traumatic event. Dramatic clinical regressions occur with some frequency. Secondary gain (favorable litigation outcome) may be a significant factor in maintaining PTSD symptoms and impairment. Another reason why PTSD claimants generally do poorly in litigation is the adversarial context. Among friends or in therapy, the PTSD patient receives support and empathy. The traumatic experience is validated. Empathy provides a powerfully healing experience. In litigation, an aggressive attempt is made to invalidate the traumatic experience and subsequent psychological response of the PTSD claimant. Dramatic worsening of the PTSD claimant's psychological condition can occur.

A number of factors must be considered by the forensic examiner when he or she is called on to make statements about prognosis and future needs of the litigant for treatment (see Table 3–8). These opinions need to be

grounded in available scientific data. For example, the psychiatric literature indicates that behavior therapy and medications are more effective for
intrusive symptoms, whereas psychodynamic therapy, both individual and
group, are more useful for symptoms of avoidance and social isolation
(Green 1992). Prognostic statements are more credible that analyze factors
in the PTSD litigant's personality and life situation that both favor and im-
pede clinical improvement. Inappropriate treatment obviously worsens
prognosis. Realistic therapy goals aimed at restoring functional capacity
rather than eliminating all symptoms will make for a shorter, more effective
treatment and not burden the patient-litigant with an impossible task.

The length of treatment often depends on the treatment philosophy
and approach of the treating psychiatrist. Because usually it is difficult to
give an informed opinion about the actual length of time needed for future
treatment, a range should be given. It is perfectly appropriate to testify that
"I don't know" when reliable clinical data on which to form a reasonable
opinion are unavailable.

The following clinical vignette demonstrates the use of standard methods of assessment of functional psychiatric impairment:

> A 42-year-old landscape contractor accidentally cuts an underground
> electrical cable with a post hole digger. He is electrically shocked and
> knocked to the ground. There is no loss of consciousness. He is hospital-
> ized briefly for observation. PTSD symptoms develop within a week of the
> accident. Recurrent flashbacks and nightmares of the traumatic event are
> prominent. He withdraws from his family and friends.
>
> On examination 1 year later, his activities of daily living have resumed
> and are normal. He returned to full time work 3 months after the acci-
> dent. His relationship with family and friends has returned to preincident

Table 3–8. Factors influencing the prognosis of a litigant with posttraumatic stress disorder (PTSD)

- ❏ Dose level of trauma
- ❏ Susceptibility (preexisting psychiatric history)
- ❏ Acuteness or chronicity of symptoms at time of evaluation
- ❏ Motivation for treatment
- ❏ Appropriate treatment
- ❏ Availability of personal and social support
- ❏ "Litogenic" (status of litigation)

levels. Golf and tennis are enjoyed again. As the time of trial approaches, however, flashbacks and nightmares recur that have been quiescent for 6 months.

The examiner, using Axis V of DSM-IV and the AMA *Guides to Evaluation of Permanent Impairment,* finds mild impairment in functioning. Using the AMA *Guides to the Evaluation of Permanent Impairment,* the forensic examiner generally finds concentration to be good. Activities of daily living show no permanent impairment. Social functioning has returned to nearly preincident levels. Persistence (staying power to complete tasks) is good. Pace (finishing tasks in a timely manner) is unimpaired. The ability to manage stress without deterioration or decompensation (adaption) is normal except when litigation issues arise. A recrudescence of brief, low-intensity flashbacks and occasional nightmares secondary to the litigation produce temporary, moderate anxiety and withdrawal from relationships. The forensic examiner concludes that the claimant's overall impairment is mild (class 2).

Also using DSM-IV Axis 5 Global Assessment of Functioning Scale (GAF Scale), a rating is made for two time periods: current (time of examination) and past year (highest level of functioning for at least a few months during the past year) (American Psychiatric Association 1994, p. 30). [In DSM-IV, the evaluation of GAF during the past year is made optional. For PTSD claimants whose symptoms have existed for more than 1 year, preincident functional assessment also should be performed. The current GAF generally reflects the present need for treatment or care. The highest GAF has prognostic significance because an individual usually returns to a previous level of functioning after an episode of illness.] The forensic examiner rates the current GAF at 80 (mild impairment) and the highest GAF at 90 (slight impairment). The lower current GAF rating reflects mild exacerbation of PTSD symptoms paralleling increased activity in the litigation process.

Proposed Guideline

Standard assessment methods should be used in evaluating the level of functional psychological impairment of PTSD claimants. Relying solely on clinical experience or on strictly subjective or idiosyncratic criteria in assessing psychological impairment should be avoided.

Conclusion

The DSM-IV, published in early 1994, is the primary diagnostic reference manual into the twenty-first century. DSM-IV contains expanded diagnostic criteria for PTSD that may prove even more problematic in the legal context. The evolution of guidelines for the forensic psychiatric evaluation of PTSD claimants may assist in preventing misuse of this diagnosis in litigation.

The development of guidelines for the forensic psychiatric examination of PTSD claimants will help ensure fairness to all parties in litigation. A credible forensic examination will assist meritorious claims of PTSD while also protecting defendants against spurious claims. Thereby, those who are truly injured will be appropriately compensated. Defendants, including insurers, also will have the confidence that they have received fair protection from unwarranted claims.

References

American Academy of Psychiatry and the Law: Ethical Guidelines for the Practice of Forensic Psychiatry. Adopted May 1987—Revised October 1989 and 1991. Baltimore, MD, American Academy of Psychiatry and the Law, 1991

American Medical Association: Guides to the Evaluation of Permanent Impairment, 4th Edition. Chicago, IL, American Medical Association, 1993

American Psychiatric Association: Diagnostic and Statistical Manual: Mental Disorders. Washington, DC, American Psychiatric Association, 1952

American Psychiatric Association: Diagnostic and Statistical Manual of Mental Disorders, 2nd Edition. Washington, DC, American Psychiatric Association, 1968

American Psychiatric Association: Diagnostic and Statistical Manual of Mental Disorders, 3rd Edition. Washington, DC, American Psychiatric Association, 1980

American Psychiatric Association: Diagnostic and Statistical Manual of Mental Disorders, 3rd Edition, Revised. Washington, DC, American Psychiatric Association, 1987

American Psychiatric Association: Diagnostic and Statistical Manual of Mental Disorders, 4th Edition. Washington, DC, American Psychiatric Association, 1994

American Psychiatric Association Task Force on DSM-IV: DSM-IV Options Book: Washington, DC, American Psychiatric Association, 1991

Appelbaum PS, Jick RZ, Grisso T, et al: Use of posttraumatic stress disorder to support an insanity defense. Am J Psychiatry 150:229–234, 1993

Babitsky S, Sewall HD: Using the AMA Guide in cross examination. Trial Diplomacy Journal 15:47–54, 1992

Behan RC, Hirschfeld AH: The accident process; II: toward more rational treatment of industrial injuries. JAMA 186:300–306, 1963

Blank AS: The unconscious flashback to the war in Vietnam veterans: clinical mystery, legal defense, and community problem, in The Trauma of War. Edited by Sonnenberg SM, Blank AS, Talbott JA. Washington, DC, American Psychiatric Press, 1985, pp 293–308

Blank AS: The longitudinal course of posttraumatic stress disorder, in Posttraumatic Stress Disorder—DSM-IV and Beyond. Edited by Davidson JRT, Foa EB. Washington, DC, American Psychiatric Press, 1993, pp 3–22

Bremner JD, Southwick SM, Johnson DR, et al: Childhood physical abuse and combat-related posttraumatic stress disorder in Vietnam veterans. Am J Psychiatry 150:235–239, 1993a

Bremner JD, Scott TM, Delaney RC, et al: Deficits in short-term memory in posttraumatic stress disorder. Am J Psychiatry 150:1015–1019, 1993b

Bremner JD, Davis M, Southwick SM, et al: Neurobiology of posttraumatic stress disorder, in American Psychiatric Press Review of Psychiatry, Vol 12. Edited by Oldham JM, Riba MB, Tasman A. Washington, DC, American Psychiatric Press, 1993c, pp 183–204

Breslau N, Davis GC: Posttraumatic Stress Disorder in an urban population of young adults: risk factors for chronicity. Am J Psychiatry 149:671–675, 1992

Breslau N, Davis GL, Andreski P, et al: Traumatic events and posttraumatic stress disorder in an urban population of young adults. Arch Gen Psychiatry 48:216–222, 1991

Briere J, Zaida LY: Sexual abuse histories and sequelae in female psychiatric emergency room patients. Am J Psychiatry 146:1602–1607, 1989

Bryer JB, Nelson BA, Miller JB, et al: Childhood sexual and physical abuse as factors in adult psychiatric illness. Am J Psychiatry 144:1426–1430, 1987

Burstein A: Post-traumatic stress disorder. J Clin Psychiatry 46:300–301, 1985

Charney DS, Deutch AY, Krystal JH, et al: Psychobiologic mechanisms of posttraumatic stress disorder. Arch Gen Psychiatry 50:294–305, 1993

Cohen RE: Twenty Years and Twenty Post-trauma Clinical Lessons: From Macro Events to Micro Application. American Psychiatric Association's Simon Bolivar Lecture. Presented at the 145th Annual Meeting of the American Psychiatric Association, Washington, DC, May 4, 1992

Cottler LB, Compton WM, Mager D, et al: Posttraumatic stress disorder among substance users from the general population. Am J Psychiatry 149:664–670, 1992

Davidson J: Issue in the diagnosis of posttraumatic stress disorder, in American Psychiatric Press Review of Psychiatry, Vol 12. Edited by Oldham JM, Riba MB, Tasman A. Washington, DC, American Psychiatric Press, 1993, pp 141–155

Davidson JRT: Clinical efficacy shown in pharmacologic treatment of post-traumatic stress disorder. The Psychiatric Times, September 1991, pp 62–63

Davidson JRT, Fairbanks JA: The epidemiology of posttraumatic stress disorder, in Posttraumatic Stress Disorder—DSM-IV and Beyond. Edited by Davidson JRT, Foa EB. Washington, DC, American Psychiatric Press, 1993, pp 147–189

Davidson JRT, Foa EB: Diagnostic issues in posttraumatic stress disorder: considerations for DSM-IV. J Abnorm Psychol 100:346–355, 1991

Davidson JRT, Smith RD, Kudler HS: Validity and reliability of DSM-III criteria for posttraumatic stress disorder: experience with a structured interview. J Nerv Ment Dis 177:336–341, 1989

Davidson JRT, Kudler HS, Saunders WE, et al: Symptom and morbidity patterns in World War II and Vietnam veterans with post-traumatic stress disorder. Compr Psychiatry 31:1662–1670, 1990a

Davidson JRT, Kudler HS, Smith RD, et al: Treatment of posttraumatic stress disorder with amitriptyline and placebo. Arch Gen Psychiatry 47:259–266, 1990b

Dohmann v Richard, 282 So2d 789 (La Ct App 1973)

Embry CK: Psychotherapeutic interventions in chronic posttraumatic stress disorder, in Posttraumatic Stress Disorder: Etiology, Phenomenology, and Treatment. Edited by Wolf ME, Mosnaim AD. Washington, DC, American Psychiatric Press, 1990, pp 226–236

Enelow AJ: Psychiatric disorders and work function. Psychiatric Annals 21:27–35, 1991

Epstein RS: Avoidant symptoms cloaking the diagnosis of PTSD in patients with severe accidental injury. Journal of Traumatic Stress 6:451–473, 1993

Eth S, Pynoos RS (eds): Post-Traumatic Stress Disorder in Children. Washington, DC, American Psychiatric Press, 1985

Ethics Committee of the American Psychiatric Association: The Principles of Medical Ethics: With Annotations Especially Applicable to Psychiatry. Washington, DC, American Psychiatric Association, 1992

Frances AJ: Conceptual problems of psychiatric classification. Presented at the annual meeting of the American Psychiatric Association, New York, New York, May 15, 1990

Gammons v Osteopathic Hospital of Maine, Inc., 534 A2d 1282, 1285 (Me 1987)

Gleser G, Green BL, Winget C: Prolonged Psychosocial Effects of Disaster: A Study of Buffalo Creek. New York, Academic Press, 1981

Goldman HH, Skodol AE, Lave TR: Revising Axis V for DSM-IV: a review of measurers of social functioning. Am J Psychiatry 149:1148–1156, 1992

Goldstein G, van Kammen W, Shelly C, et al: Survivors of imprisonment in the Pacific Theater during World War II. Am J Psychiatry 144:1210–1213, 1987

Goodwin DW, Guze SB: Anxiety neurosis (panic disorder), in Psychiatric Diagnosis, 3rd Edition. New York, Oxford University Press, 1984

Green BL: Assessing the levels of psychiatric impairment following disaster. J Nerv Ment Dis 170:544–552, 1982

Green BL: New Research: Implications for the Diagnosis of PTSD. Panel Discussion at The Development of Standards for the Forensic Examination of Post-traumatic Stress Disorder Claimants. Washington, DC, Georgetown University, November 19, 1992

Green BL, Wilson JP, Lindy JD: Conceptualizing post-traumatic stress disorder: a psychosocial framework, in Trauma and Its Wake: The Study and Treatment of Post-Traumatic Stress Disorder. Edited by Figley CR. New York, Brunner/Mazel, 1985a, pp 53–69

Green BL, Grace MC, Gleser GC: Identifying survivors at risk: long-term impairment following the Beverly Hills Supper Club Fire. J Consult Clin Psychol 53:672–678, 1985b

Green BL, Lindy JD, Grace MC: Post-traumatic stress disorder: toward DSM-IV. J Nerv Ment Dis 173:406–411, 1985c

Green BL, Lindy JD, Grace ML, et al: Buffalo Creek survivors in the second decade: stability of stress symptoms. Am J Orthopsychiatry 60:43–54, 1990a

Green BL, Grace MC, Lindy JD, et al: Buffalo Creek survivors in the second decade: comparison with unexposed and nonlitigant groups. Journal of Applied Social Psychology 20:1033–1050, 1990b

Guidelines for Handling Psychiatric Issues in Workers' Compensation Cases. Rancho Palos Verdes, Ca, Lex-Com Enterprises, p 5, 1988

Gunderson JG, Sabo AN: The phenomenological and conceptual interface between borderline personality disorder and PTSD. Am J Psychiatry 150:19–27, 1993

Helzer JE, Robins LN, McEvoy L: Posttraumatic stress disorder in the general population. N Engl J Med 317:1630–1634, 1987

Hendin H, Haas AP, Singer P: The reliving experience in Vietnam veterans with posttraumatic stress disorder. Compr Psychiatry 25:167–173, 1984

Herman JL: Trauma and Recovery. New York, Basic Books, 1992

Herman JL: Sequelae of prolonged and repeated trauma: evidence for a complex posttraumatic syndrome (DESNOS), in Posttraumatic Stress Disorder—DSM-IV and Beyond. Edited by Davidson JRT, Foa EB. Washington, DC, American Psychiatric Press, 1993, pp 213–228

Herman JL, van der Kolk BA: Traumatic antecedents of borderline personality disorder, in Psychological Trauma. Edited by van der Kolk BA. Washington, DC, American Psychiatric Press, 1987, pp 111–126

Hirschfeld AH, Behan RC: The accident process; I: etiological considerations for industrial injuries. JAMA 186:193–199, 1963

Hirschfeld AH, Behan RC: The accident process; III: disability: acceptable and unacceptable. JAMA 197:125–129, 1966

Horowitz MJ: Stress Response Syndromes. New York, Jason Aronson, 1976

Horowitz MJ: Post-traumatic stress disorders. Behavioral Sciences and the Law 1:9–23, 1983

Keeton WP, Dobbs DB, Keeton RW, et al: Prosser and Keeton on the Law of Torts, 5th Edition. St Paul, MN, West Publishing, 1984, p 292

Kinzie JD: Posttraumatic stress disorder, in Comprehensive Textbook of Psychiatry, 4th Edition, Vol 1. Edited by Kaplan HI, Sadock BJ. Baltimore, MD, Williams & Wilkins, 1989, pp 1000–1008

Kionka EJ: Torts: Injuries to Persons and Property. St. Paul, MN, West, 1977, p 359

Kluznik J, Speed N, Van Valkenburg C, et al: Forty-year follow-up of United States prisoners of war. Am J Psychiatry 143:1443–1446, 1986

Koopman C, Classen C, Spiegel D: Predictors of posttraumatic stress symptoms among survivors of the Oakland/Berkeley, Calif., firestorm. Am J Psychiatry 151:888–894, 1994

Kulka RA, Schlenger WE, Fairbanks JA, et al: Trauma and the Vietnam War Generation. New York, Brunner/Mazel, 1990

Lasky H: Psychiatric disability evaluation of the injured worker: legal overview. Psychiatric Annals 21:16–22, 1991

Lowenstein RJ: An office mental status examination for complex chronic dissociative symptoms. Psychiatr Clin North Am 14:567–603, 1991a

Lowenstein RJ: Psychogenic amnesia and psychogenic fugue: a comprehensive review, in American Psychiatric Press Annual Review of Psychiatry, Vol 10. Edited by Tasman A, Goldfinger SM. Washington, DC, American Psychiatric Press, 1991b, pp 189–222

Lystad M (ed): Mental Response to Mass Emergencies. New York, Brunner/Mazel, 1988

March JS: What constitutes a stressor? The "criterion A" issue in PTSD, in Posttraumatic Stress Disorder—DSM-IV and Beyond. Edited by Davidson JRT, Foa EB. Washington, DC, American Psychiatric Press, 1993, pp 37–54

Marmar CR, Foy D, Kagan B, et al: An integrated approach for treating posttraumatic stress, in American Psychiatric Press Review of Psychiatry, Vol 12. Edited by Oldham JM, Riba MB, Tasman A. Washington, DC, American Psychiatric Press, 1993, pp 239–272

Marsella AJ, Freidman MJ, Spain EH: Ethnocultural aspects of posttraumatic stress disorder, in American Psychiatric Press Review of Psychiatry, Vol 12. Edited by Oldham JM, Riba MB, Tasman A. Washington, DC, American Psychiatric Press, 1993, pp 157–181

McAllister TW: Mild traumatic brain injury and the postconcussive syndrome, in Neuropsychiatry of Traumatic Brain Injury. Edited by Silver JM, Yudofsky SC, Hales RE. Washington, DC, American Psychiatric Press, 1994, pp 357–392

McFarlane AC: The Phenomenology of posttraumatic stress disorders following a natural disaster. J Nerv Ment Dis 176:22–29, 1988

McFarlane AC: The aetiology of posttraumatic morbidity: predisposing, precipitating and perpetuating factors. Br J Psychiatry 154:221–228, 1989

McFarlane AC: Vulnerability to posttraumatic stress disorder, in Posttraumatic Stress Disorder: Etiology, Phenomenology, and Treatment. Edited by Wolf ME, Mosnaim AD. Washington, DC, American Psychiatric Press, 1990, pp 2–20

McGee R: Flashbacks and memory phenomena. J Nerv Ment Dis 172:273–278, 1984

Mellman TA, Randolph CA, Brawman-Mintzer O, et al: Phenomenology and course of psychiatric disorders associated with combat-related posttraumatic stress disorder. Am J Psychiatry 149:1568–1574, 1992

Meyerson AT, Fine T (eds): Psychiatric Disability: Clinical, Legal and Administrative Dimensions. Washington, DC, American Psychiatric Press, 1987

Nagy LM, Morgan CA, Southwick SM, et al: Open prospective trial of fluoxetine for posttraumatic stress disorder. J Clin Psychopharmacol 13:107–113, 1993

Nally RJ, Saigh PA: On the distinction between traumatic simple phobia and posttraumatic stress disorder, in Posttraumatic Stress Disorder—DSM-IV and Beyond. Edited by Davidson JRT, Foa EB. Washington, DC, American Psychiatric Press, 1993, pp 207–212

Panzarella JP: The nature of work, job loss, and the diagnostic complexities of the psychologically injured worker. Psychiatric Annals 21:10–15, 1991

Perr IN: Claims of psychiatric injury after alleged false arrest. J Forensic Sci 33:21–34, 1988

Perr IN: Asbestos exposure and post-traumatic stress disorder. Bull Am Acad Psychiatry Law 21:3:331–344, 1993

Perry S, Difede MA, Musngi G, et al: Predictors of posttraumatic stress disorder after burn injury. Am J Psychiatry 149:931–935, 1992

Pilowsky I: Minor accidents and major psychological trauma: a clinical perspective. Stress Medicine 8:77–78, 1992

Pitman RK: Biological findings in posttraumatic stress disorder: implications for DSM-IV classification, in Posttraumatic Stress Disorder—DSM-IV and Beyond. Edited by Davidson JRT, Foa EB. Washington, DC, American Psychiatric Press, 1993, pp 173–189

Pitman RK, Orr SP: Psychophysiologic testing for post-traumatic stress disorder: forensic psychiatric application. Bull Am Acad Psychiatry Law 21:37–52, 1993

Pitman RK, Saunders LS, Orr SP: Psychophysiologic testing for posttraumatic stress disorder. Trial, April 1994, pp 22–26

Pynoos RS: Traumatic stress and developmental psychopathology in children and adolescents, in American Psychiatric Press Review of Psychiatry, Vol 12. Edited by Oldham JM, Riba MB, Tasman A. Washington, DC, American Psychiatric Press, 1993, pp 205–238

Raifman LJ: Problems of diagnosis and legal causation in courtroom use of post-traumatic stress disorder. Behavioral Sciences and the Law 1:115–130, 1983

Reich JH: Personality disorders and posttraumatic stress disorder, in Posttraumatic Stress Disorder: Etiology, Phenomenology, and Treatment. Edited by Wolf ME, Mosnaim AD. Washington, DC, American Psychiatric Press, 1990, pp 64–79

Robins LN, Helzer JE, Croughan J, et al: National Institute of Mental Health Diagnostic Interview Schedule. Arch Gen Psychiatry 38:381–389, 1981

Roca RP, Spence RJ, Munster AM: Posttraumatic adaptation and distress among adult burn survivors. Am J Psychiatry 149:1234–1238, 1992

Ross CA: Epidemiology of multiple personality disorder and dissociation. Psychiatr Clin North Am 14:567–603, 1991

Rothbaum BO, Foa EB: Subtypes of posttraumatic stress disorder and duration of symptoms, in Posttraumatic Stress Disorder—DSM-IV and Beyond. Edited by Davidson JRT, Foa EB. Washington, DC, American Psychiatric Press, 1993, pp 23–35

Rothbaum BO, Foa EB, Riggs DS, et al: A prospective examination of post-traumatic stress disorder in rape victims. Journal of Traumatic Stress 5:455–475, 1992

Sales E, Baum M, Shore B: Victim readjustment following assault. Journal of Social Issues 40:117–136, 1984

Salley v Childs, 541 A2d 1297, 1300 n 4 (Me 1988)

Schottenfeld RS, Cullen MR: Occupation-induced posttraumatic stress disorders. Am J Psychiatry 142:198–202, 1985

Scrignar CB: PTSD: Diagnosis, Treatment and Legal Issues, 2nd Edition. New Orleans, LA, Bruno Press, 1988

Selye H: The Physiology and Pathology of Exposure to Stress. Montreal, Canada, Acta, 1950

Simon RI: Cancerphobia: myth or malady in psychic injury litigation. Trauma 29:43–60, 1988

Simon RI: Clinical Psychiatry and the Law, 2nd Edition. Washington, DC, American Psychiatric Press, 1992a

Simon RI: Ethical and legal issues, in American Psychiatric Press Textbook of Neuropsychiatry, 2nd Edition. Edited by Yudofsky SC, Hales RE. Washington, DC, American Psychiatric Press, 1992b, pp 793–805

Simon RI: Ethical and legal issues, in Neuropsychiatry of Traumatic Brain Injury. Edited by Silver JM, Yudofsky SC, Hales RE. Washington, DC, American Psychiatric Press, 1994a, pp 569–627

Simon RI: The law and psychiatry, in The American Psychiatric Press Textbook of Psychiatry, 2nd Edition. Edited by Hales RE, Yudofsky SC, Talbott JA. Washington, DC, American Psychiatric Press, 1994b, pp 1297–1340

Slovenko R: Legal aspects of post-traumatic stress disorder. Psychiatr Clin North Am 17:439–446, 1994

Southwick SM, Yehuda R, Giller EL: Personality disorders in treatment-seeking combat: veterans with posttraumatic stress disorder. Am J Psychiatry 150:1020–1023, 1993a

Southwick SM, Krystal JH, Morgan CA, et al: Abnormal nonadrenergic function in posttraumatic stress disorder. Arch Gen Psychiatry 50:266–274, 1993b

Sparr LF: Legal aspects of posttraumatic stress disorder: uses and abuses, in Posttraumatic Stress Disorder: Etiology, Phenomenology, and Treatment. Edited by Wolf ME, Mosnaim AD. Washington, DC, American Psychiatric Press, 1990, pp 234–264

Sparr LF, Boehnlein JK: Posttraumatic stress disorder in tort actions: forensic minefield. Bull Am Acad Psychiatry Law 18:283–302, 1990

Spaulding WJ: Compensation for mental disability, in Psychiatry, Vol 3. Edited by Cavenar JO. Philadelphia, PA, Lippincott, 1991, pp 1–27

Spencer v General Electric Co, 688 F Supp 1072, ED VA 1988

Spiegel D: Dissociation and trauma, in American Psychiatric Press Review of Psychiatry, Vol 10. Edited by Tasman A, Goldfinger SM. Washington, DC, American Psychiatric Press, 1991, pp 261–275

Spiegel D, Cardeña E: Dissociative mechanisms in posttraumatic stress disorder, in Posttraumatic Stress Disorder: Etiology, Phenomenology, and Treatment. Edited by Wolf ME, Mosnaim AD. Washington, DC, American Psychiatric Press, 1990, pp 22–34

State v Kim, 64 HAW 598, 645 P2d 1130, 1982

Sterling v Velsicol Chemical Corp, 855 F2d 1188 (6th Cir 1988)

Stone AA: Post-traumatic stress disorder and the law: critical review of the new frontier. Bull Am Acad Psychiatry Law 21:23–36, 1993

Strasburger LH: "Crudely, without any finesse": the defendant hears his psychiatric evaluation. Bull Am Acad Psychiatry Law 15:229–233, 1987

Sutker PB, Winstead DK, Galina ZH, et al: Cognitive deficits and psychopathology among former prisoners of war and combat veterans of the Korean conflict. Am J Psychiatry 148:62–72, 1991

Sutker PB, Allain AN, Winstead DK: Psychopathology and psychiatric diagnoses of World War II Pacific Theater prisoner of war survivors and combat veterans. Am J Psychiatry 150:240–245, 1993

Sutherland SM, Davidson JRT: Pharmacotherapy for post-traumatic stress disorder. Psychiatr Clin North Am 17:409–423, 1994

Terr L: Chowchilla revisited: the effects of psychic trauma four years after a school bus kidnapping. Am J Psychiatry 140:1543–1550, 1983

Theriaulta v Swan, 558 A2d 369, 372 (Me 1989)

Tomb DA: The phenomenology of post-traumatic stress disorder. Psychiatr Clin North Am 17:237–250, 1994

Trimble MR: Post-Traumatic Neurosis: From Railway Spine to the Whiplash. New York, Wiley, 1981

True WR, Rice J, Eisen SA, et al: A twin study of genetic and environmental contributions to liability for posttraumatic stress symptoms. Arch Gen Psychiatry 50:257–264, 1993

van der Kolk BA: The psychological consequences of overwhelming life experiences, in Psychological Trauma. Edited by van der Kolk BA. Washington, DC, American Psychiatric Press, 1987, pp 1–30

van der Kolk B, Blitz R, Burr W, et al: Nightmares and trauma: a comparison of nightmares after combat with lifelong nightmares in veterans. Am J Psychiatry 141:187–190, 1984

Van Putten T, Emory WH: Traumatic neurosis in Vietnam returnees—a forgotten diagnosis? Arch Gen Psychiatry 29:695–698, 1973

Walker JI: Vietnam combat veterans with legal difficulties: a psychiatric problem. Am J Psychiatry 138:1384–1385, 1981

Wolfe J, Keane TM: Diagnostic validity of posttraumatic stress disorder, in Posttraumatic Stress Disorder: Etiology, Phenomenology, and Treatment. Edited by Wolf ME, Mosnaim AD. Washington, DC, American Psychiatric Press, 1990, pp 48–63

Zebo v Houston, 800 P2d 245 (Okla 1990)

Chapter 4

Guidelines for the Psychiatric Examination of Posttraumatic Stress Disorder in Children and Adolescents

Kathleen M. Quinn, M.D.

The DSM-III-R (American Psychiatric Association 1987) was the first diagnostic manual to officially recognize posttraumatic stress disorder (PTSD) as a diagnosis applicable to children. However, men and women of letters have described symptoms of reexperiencing, avoidance, and emotional constriction secondary to childhood trauma for hundreds of years. Samuel Pepys, a victim of the Great London Fire, wrote of symptoms consistent with PTSD (Daly 1983) in 1666. Richard Rhodes, an acclaimed author, described traumatic childhood dreams related to the experience of severe abuse and neglect at the hands of a stepmother (Rhodes 1990). Virginia Woolf described nightmares attributed to sexual abuse as a child (Terr 1990).

The study and description of PTSD is based primarily on clinical and empirical studies of adults exposed to natural and man-made disasters beginning with the reports of "traumatic neurosis" among combat soldiers in World War I. The application of PTSD symptoms to children in DSM-III-R consisted of a downward extension of diagnostic criteria of an adult disorder; this application also occurred with major depressive disorder. Earlier assumptions that children exposed to trauma had less serious and more transient reactions than adults (Benedek 1985) were revised in DSM-III-R in the face of clinical studies of children exposed to a wide range of traumas (Newman 1976; Terr 1979; Pynoos and Eth 1985). DSM-IV (American Psychiatric Association 1994) reflects such a greater sensitivity to developmental variations by recognizing that some diagnostic criteria may vary in nature and degree in minors as compared with adults. As the study of PTSD in minors becomes more rigorous, so too must the guidelines of forensic assessment of PTSD in children and adolescents. This chapter addresses relevant historical trends, epidemiology, the psychiatric morbidity in traumatized children and adolescents, and the structure and content of the forensic examination of such minors.

History

Sigmund Freud (1926/1959) formulated one of the first theories of psychic trauma, noting that in a traumatic situation "external and internal, real and instinctual dangers converge." He also called specific attention to child witnesses, including children who observed parental sexual intercourse, which, Freud posited, might be experienced as a traumatic situation (S. Freud 1918/1959). However, this work was based on adult retrospective reporting and reconstruction of childhood experiences.

Work directly with children did not begin until the 1940s when Anna Freud and Burlingham (1943) published anecdotal material about young children in World War II and Levy (1945) studied children undergoing surgical procedures. Freud and Burlingham emphasized the importance of the impact of parental loss as well as the importance of the parents' role as a buffer to trauma. Levy's work described 25% of children postsurgery as having emotional sequelae similar to those in adults with combat neurosis, with the largest number of symptoms in children younger than 3 years of age. Subsequent early studies (Bloch 1956; Burke 1982) relied on general instruments completed by parents or observers and likely underestimated the prevalence of children's reactions.

As interest grew in adult trauma after the Vietnam War, so too did the study of psychic trauma in children. A wide range of events have now been studied, including disasters, kidnapping, and violence. Three studies between 1972 and 1983 indicated that children may show effects 2 to 4 years after some highly stressful disasters (Gleser et al. 1981; Lacey 1972; Terr 1979).

Epidemiology

Approximately 1% of adults qualify for a PTSD diagnosis at some time during their lifetime, whereas an additional 15% have experienced significant symptoms (Helzer et al. 1987). However, no similar estimates are available for children and adolescents. Numerous stressors place minors at risk for PTSD. For example, natural disasters are ubiquitous. Intrafamilial violence is another major source. Each year over 1 million children suffer observable harm as a result of abuse or neglect. Estimates of sexual abuse during childhood range from 1 of 5 to 2 of 5 for adult women and 1 of 10 for adult men. Furthermore, according to several estimates, more than 3 million children witness spouse abuse annually.

Recent interest has focused on children witnessing extreme violence both in their homes and in their neighborhoods. In 1990 there were over 24,000 homicides in the United States. Between 10% and 20% of all homicides are witnessed by minors. Similarly, children may be exposed to sexual assaults or suicidal behaviors of others. Increased community violence has, in some urban areas, exposed children to warlike conditions. Finally, children in war-torn countries are at especially high risk for developing PTSD symptoms.

PTSD may also develop after life-threatening illnesses, injury, or invasive medical procedures (Eth and Pynoos 1985).

Recent analysis of data from four disasters shows that the incidence of PTSD was 0%–37% according to DSM-III-R criteria (Pynoos and Nader 1989). Children often have significant symptoms but do not meet the full criteria for the PTSD diagnosis (Vogel and Vernberg 1992).

Psychiatric Outcome in Traumatized Children

The key factor affecting initial posttraumatic reactions is the degree of exposure to the stressor. The objective magnitude of the stressor is directly proportional to the risk of developing PTSD (March 1990). Exposure to life-threatening or grotesque scenes of destruction increases the probability of severe postdisaster responses. This finding has been confirmed in studies of both adults (Shore et al. 1986) and children (Gleser et al. 1981; Pynoos et al. 1987). However, the risk of PTSD is also influenced by the children's perception of the events (Schwarz and Kowalski 1991). For children, immediate life threat, presence in the impact zone, severe injury, and death or injury of family members are factors significantly associated with postdisaster emotional disturbance, including PTSD. Property damage appears related to short-term reactions after disasters but appears to have less long-term effect.

Other factors that influence outcome include the following: 1) the children's appraisal of life threat, 2) the degree of human accountability, 3) separation from significant others, 4) the presence of emotional guilt, and 5) the presence of multiple losses or disruptions in the child's life. The very young child may be partially protected because he or she does not understand the danger. Parents' or siblings' actions and words may influence the child's perceptions of the events. PTSD rates are higher in traumatic acts caused by others than in natural disasters. Separation from significant others is often an additional source of stress. Guilt may act as an independent variable that increases the risk of PTSD. For example, particular experiences such as hearing a cry for help or watching someone bleed to death may intensify guilt. However, guilt is not well studied in children. Multiple losses after a major stressor can have an additive effect and thus increase symptoms.

Individual characteristics of the child may also influence outcome and symptom expression. For example, preexisting psychopathology and previous loss and trauma are associated with more severe and prolonged symptoms. Younger children are more likely to reflect the reactions of the adults around them (Carey-Trefzer 1949; Green et al. 1991), whereas the symptoms of older children and adolescents reflect more of their own experience of the disaster. Some studies have demonstrated more PTSD symptoms in latency-age and adolescent girls than in boys of these same ages (Green et al. 1991).

Children in general are more likely than adults to develop sleep disturbances after experiencing trauma. Sleep disturbances are often secondarily associated with problems in attention and academic performance. Young children are frequently unable to express denial/avoidance or the emotional numbing symptoms of PTSD, although these symptoms are often present.

Intervening variables may strongly influence the strength and course of the child's PTSD symptoms. Symptoms in parents and in children exposed to trauma are highly correlated. Family and parental functioning are major mediating factors in a child's response to stressors. Four parental responses are associated with the persistence of symptoms in children (Pynoos 1990): 1) excessive dependence on children for support, 2) overprotectiveness, 3) preexisting parental psychopathology, and 4) negative attitude to either temporary regression in the child or open communication about the event. However, positive family functioning can ameliorate the effects of psychic trauma.

The larger community also can be an important factor. A community may suffer severe disruption or be an important, supportive influence. Teachers may be significant figures of support for a traumatized child. Children may also reflect teachers' reactions (Kliman 1968).

The impact on peer relations also should be explored. PTSD may result in decreased interest in and enjoyment of normal activities and in feelings of estrangement from others. These symptoms may result in isolation and disruption of relationships.

The range of responses to trauma in minors parallels that of adults. The major disorders that children are likely to develop include PTSD, grief, anxiety disorders, and depression (Kinzie et al. 1986; Shore et al. 1986). For example, in Kinzie's study of Cambodian adolescent refugees, 50% developed PTSD, 37% were intermittently depressed, 12% were diagnosed with major depressive disorder, and 18% were diagnosed with generalized anxiety disorder. Significant comorbidity was documented. Pynoos et al.'s (1987) 14-month follow-up of school-age children exposed to a sniper incident showed a distribution similar to that found in the Kinzie study but with more frequent separation anxiety disorder, likely due to the younger children involved in the study.

Different factors in the traumatic incident are correlated with the frequency of specific symptoms. Life threat and witnessing injury and death are highly correlated with the onset of PTSD. The loss of a significant other is associated with grief, depression, or adjustment reaction. Worry about or a sudden separation from a significant other is correlated with persistent anxiety about others.

In addition to the DSM-IV formal criteria, studies have indicated that children often have other symptoms, such as increased somatic complaints, school absences, and decreased school performance. Specific factors unique to the trauma may exacerbate symptoms such as time skews or distortions. For example, the time distortions described by Terr (1979) in the Chowchilla victims may be related to their long period of time spent in the dark at the beginning of the kidnapping and their captivity in an underground site.

Debate continues as to whether children and adolescents are more susceptible to the development of PTSD than adults. Andreasen (1985) found a significantly higher rate of PTSD in children than in adults 1 year after they received severe burns. However, Schwarz and Kowalski (1991) found similar PTSD symptoms in both adults and children who were screened after a school shooting. Most evidence indicates that early responses to trauma predict later symptomatology in both school-age children and adolescents just as they do in adults.

The Role of the Forensic Clinician

The first task of the forensic clinician asked to evaluate an allegedly traumatized minor is to clarify the scope and focus of the evaluation. Is the clinician being asked to investigate the allegations? Is the focus a description of the extent of the damages? Are questions of liability to be addressed? The clinician must establish the feasibility of accepting the referral and his or her expertise to do so. For example, investigations of allegations are preferably done early after the disclosure or event. Entrance into such a case must be coordinated with mandated investigators (protective services and/or police) in abuse cases. If an investigation is pursued, the clinician must anticipate scrutiny of his or her methods as well as the child's disclosure and carefully plan the structure of the evaluation.

Evaluations aimed at describing damages and/or liability are best done by experienced forensic clinicians. If prepubertal children are to be examined, the evaluator should have formal child training. The forensic evaluation of traumatized children should be separated from ongoing therapy to protect therapeutic alliances and to avoid charges of bias or venality.

Forensic clinicians must scrutinize cases for factors that may cause over- and underidentification of trauma in children. Many factors prevent the recognition of trauma in minors. Parents, teachers, and clinicians often deny or minimize the impact of distressing events on children. Denial by adults may be based on their conflict over their inability to protect children. Adults may also fail to appreciate the frequency of trauma in children's lives. Children often do not report traumatic events. For example, in Russell's (1986) study, only 2% of women sexually abused during childhood reported intrafamilial abuse as minors.

Recent trends may cause overidentification of "trauma" and its impact. Low standards of mandatory reporting acts and cadres of victimologists may lead to false positive identification of trauma. Incomplete or biased exams may lead to the false imputation of all symptoms to a traumatic event, with inadequate exploration of past history and functioning or of other past stressors.

Forensic clinicians embarking on these exams need to maintain a developmental perspective. Green (1991) and colleagues propose a model of children's processing of a traumatic event that can also be used to structure a forensic exam. What are the characteristics of the stressor? How does the child cognitively process the event? What are the characteristics of the children and of the environment that will affect the child's reactions and subsequent adjustment?

A developmental focus will also alert the clinician to the variation of PTSD symptoms with age. Intrusive recollections in children are more likely to be single images or sounds related to the immediate threat or injury. A child's language may be limited or idiosyncratic, leading to a sparseness in his or her reported symptoms. The use of art or role-play may be helpful in detailing the child's perceptions, but great care must be taken to avoid leading or suggestive questioning by the evaluator. Similarly, traumatic dreams in children are often short and unelaborated depictions of the trauma. These dreams may occur in stage 2 or 4 sleep rather than during REM, leading to motor restlessness, agitation, or cries of fear while asleep. After a short time, dreams may be transformed to general nightmares of monsters, of rescuing others, or of other catastrophes threatening self or others. Traumatic dreams may lengthen the course of PTSD because of heightened anxiety, or they may cause secondary problems such as the child's sleeping with his or her parents. The forensic evaluator should ask the parent and child separately about sleep routines and the frequency and content of nightmares before and after the trauma.

The forensic clinician should remember that repetitive play related to the trauma is the hallmark of traumatized children. The play may include scenes of murder, rape, or suicide. The traumatized child may include or enlist siblings or peers in the play. PTSD symptoms may also evolve. For example, as intrusive recollections are incorporated into play, these thoughts may decrease. Parents may be better able to report posttraumatic play than the children themselves (K. Nadar and R. S. Pynoos, unpublished observations, 1991).

The presence of reenactment behavior should be assessed by the forensic clinician. Reenactment behavior is defined as repetition of some part of a traumatic experience and is recognized as a diagnostic criterion in DSM-IV. In younger children, the behavior may be *action memory* (Terr 1988), such as a preschooler who had been trapped in a well who after the event ended began to squeeze himself into small places. These behaviors may include efforts to offset in action original moments of traumatic helplessness. Reenactment can also include severe risk-taking and danger. Adolescents who have access to guns, automobiles, or substances may place themselves in life-threatening situations.

The developmental perspective will also inform the forensic clinician that children's distress at traumatic reminders is triggered by more concrete reminders than is the distress of adults. Such distress appears as frequently in children as in adults. A more difficult symptom to assess is psychological numbing and avoidance (Green 1991). These symptoms may not be endorsed by children but may be observed by parents and teachers. However, parents too are often unaware of their child's sense of aloneness. Clinically, children may experience an inhibition in spontaneous thought and imagination to avoid generating any reminders. School work and social activities may suffer. DSM-III-R and DSM-IV required more symptoms of avoidance than DSM-III; fewer children have met these avoidance criteria.

The forensic clinician should assess the child for memory disturbances secondary to the trauma. Initially, clinical studies suggested a relative absence of major amnesia in children, but recent studies have demonstrated a variety of memory disturbances including 1) omitting moments of extreme life threat; 2) distorting the proximity, duration, or sequence of events; 3) experiencing omens or premonitions; and 4) minimizing life threat. In the clinical history and interview, the clinician should look for the presence of dissociative memory disturbances, which occur especially in response to physical coercion or sexual assault.

The examination should document the presence or absence of the loss of developmental skills in response to the stressors. Younger children may become less verbal, at times mute. Enuresis, clinginess, and thumbsucking may appear or increase. School-age children may appear less consistent in behavior, mood, and action. Adolescents may appear overwhelmed, with impaired decision making.

Many clinicians have described a change in orientation to the future in traumatized children. Victims may describe a sense of foreshortened future and negative or altered expectations concerning attitudes toward marriage, career, and children. Such symptoms may be a way to avoid addressing the initial trauma by concentrating on new fears. Controversy remains as to whether these symptoms are more common in adults or children.

Lastly, the forensic clinician should explore the presence of increased states of arousal, which are frequent in traumatized children and can include sleep disturbances, hypervigilance, and increased startle response. Fears are especially evident, especially at times of increased vulnerability (e.g., at bedtime, at court appearances) or with specific reminders. Children may also exhibit difficulty modulating aggression, which can be temporary or chronic, leading to irritability or overt acts.

Prognosis of PTSD

The forensic evaluator is often asked to form an opinion concerning the prognosis of a child with PTSD. The clinical course of PTSD is highly variable. Prognosis is dependent on the nature of the stressor, the characteristics of the child, and external intervening factors. The more severe the stress in intensity, duration, suddenness, or personal impact, the more prolonged the course. If the stressor includes mild exposure and minimal personal impact, symptoms often diminish within weeks of the event. A brief, immediate, intense reaction after a traumatic event may result in acute stress disorder, as described in DSM-IV. Mildly to moderately exposed children are most likely to report intrusive reexperiencing (Jones and Ribbie 1991). A chronic course is to be expected when the child has been exposed to multiple injuries, numerous losses of life, or massive destruction. A wide range of ongoing symptoms may occur, from decreased impulse control to increased inhibition. Symptoms of avoidance and numbing as well as arousal are more likely to be evident in persons who are highly exposed to a traumatic event (Pynoos et al. 1987).

The differential diagnosis should include adjustment disorder, grief, depressive disorder, or anxiety disorder. *Contagion* or *secondary traumatization* should also be considered and is a phenomenon commonly reported in children (Lyons 1987). For example, Rosenbeck and Nathan (1985) reported on a boy who was the son of a Vietnam War veteran with PTSD. The boy showed many PTSD-like symptoms, including a preoccupation with combat games and fantasies despite no direct exposure to war. Contagion may be an especially important factor in mass disclosures or severely conflicted family cases. The forensic examiner should attempt to carefully understand the timing and nature of the initial disclosure, the degree of contamination of a child's statements by others, and the context of the family dynamics and their possible relevance to credibility of the child's statements and symptom formation.

Forensic Assessment of the Traumatized Child

A clinician accepting the forensic assessment of an allegedly traumatized child should pose these questions to him- or herself prior to accepting the case. Do I have adequate child interviewing skills? Am I knowledgeable about child development, child witness issues, and the natural history of the conditions or disorders relevant to this case (e.g., PTSD in children, sexual abuse, severe burns)? If the alleged victim is prepubertal, do I have formal child training?

If the case is accepted, the referral question must be clarified to distinguish investigation questions, liability, and damages questions. The evaluation should be structured to address the specific questions, including a plan for collateral interviews and document review. Thorough preliminary document review is needed before interviews, except in investigatory cases in which the evaluator chooses to do a "blind" interview of the allegations prior to examining the document(s) in depth. The focus of the evaluation in both document review and interviews is the reconstruction of the child and family functioning pre- and posttrauma and the degree of exposure to the trauma. A key issue in the structuring of the evaluation is the prevention of role confusion. The clinician cannot simultaneously be a therapist or advocate and a forensic clinician.

Early document review should focus on pretrauma functioning and symptoms, the quality of initial investigations and early disclosures, the quality of earlier therapeutic assessment, and the victim's response to treatment. In children and adolescents, these documents should include school, medical, mental health, hospital, police, and protective service records. Past testing may document specific learning deficits predating the injury. Documents may indicate the failure of previous treatment personnel or evaluators to do a thorough history before the injury or that they relied solely on the family's and child's self-report.

The referent should be informed that the child will be interviewed alone. If the child is very young, parents may be interviewed first. The duration and frequency of interview(s) of the child must be determined on a case-by-case basis subject to the child's capacity to tolerate the evaluation and the nature of the referral question. The child interviews should be structured to maximize the child's performance and information gathering. The setting should be child friendly, with breaks during the day to avoid fatigue, hunger, or naps. A confidentiality warning and a statement of the purpose of the examination should be made to even the very young. An initial period of unstructured contact permits the evaluator to orient to the child's language and behavior. Proceeding from current functioning questions to questions about the past is often the least threatening approach. The interview(s) must elicit current mental status examination, a detailed description of postevent symptoms, and any preexisting symptoms and/or stressors. Selective use of play techniques, including drawings, props, or reenactments, may help build rapport and aid in the child's recall and capacity to communicate. Adolescents may write answers to questions they refuse to answer verbally. However, mental modification long after the event may change or alter memory. Accounts should be compared with early disclosures and collateral sources such as police reports and other witness statements. Imagined actions at the time of the event may alter recollection. The evaluator should explore the child's recall through different senses and perspectives. The child should be directly asked about the presence or absence of PTSD symptoms and to describe the content and course of the symptoms.

A complete psychosocial and mental health history should be obtained during each parent's interview. Detailed parent interviews often reveal additional documents to be requested. A history of rescue or evacuation procedures, adult responses to the event, resulting medical needs of the child, and the child's secondary exposure to the injured or dead should be obtained from the child and separately from the parents. The evaluator should clarify the child's exposure to media coverage of the event and to other family members' symptoms or distress. The assessment should indicate the absence or presence of psychological dyssynchrony in which family members progress through recovery at different speeds.

Common Pitfalls

A common pitfall in the evaluation of traumatized children is the false attribution of all symptoms to the trauma based on either an incomplete or a biased evaluation. Similarly, the prognosis may be distorted because of an incomplete database or because of bias. Clinicians, especially treatment personnel, may become overidentified with the child as a victim or attempt to help the child by overestimating damages. Evaluators may deny the impact of trauma on the child or fail to ask questions that would elicit the existing symptoms. Inadequate review of documents predating the trauma will prevent a full reconstruction of the child's history. Biased or inept interviewing of the child will distort the data gathered by the clinician. Finally, systematic bias of experts for either side will prevent a fair assessment of the child's experience and outcome.

Guidelines for the Evaluation of the Traumatized Child

1. Qualifications of the evaluator
   a. Adequate child interviewing skills
   b. Adequate knowledge of child development
   c. Adequate knowledge of child witness issues
   d. Adequate knowledge of PTSD in minors

     e. Adequate knowledge of special issues relevant to case

     f. Formal child training if child is prepubertal

2. Role of evaluator

     a. Separation of therapeutic versus forensic roles

     b. Separation of advocacy versus forensic roles

     c. Negotiation of focus of evaluation prior to acceptance of case

3. Structure of evaluation

     a. Request for and review of all relevant documents prior to interviews

     b. Separate child and parental interviews

     c. Reconstruction through history, documents, and interviews of child and family's pre- and posttrauma functioning

     d. Complete exploration of presence or absence of PTSD in child and in family members

     e. Monitoring of potential biases to over- or underidentify trauma and its effects

4. Assessment

     a. Evaluate facts and perceptions of nature of stressor

     b. Analyze the quality of earlier investigations, evaluations, and disclosures

     c. Consider the differential diagnosis of symptoms

     d. Review the treatments and their outcome

     e. Discuss the relevant prognostic issues

References

American Psychiatric Association: Diagnostic and Statistical Manual of Mental Disorders, 3rd Edition, Revised. Washington, DC, American Psychiatric Association, 1987

American Psychiatric Association: Diagnostic and Statistical Manual of Mental Disorders, 4th Edition. Washington, DC, American Psychiatric Association, 1994

Andreasen NC: Posttraumatic stress disorder, in Comprehensive Textbook of Psychiatry, 4th Edition, Vol 1. Edited by Kaplan HI, Sadock BJ. Baltimore, MD, Williams & Wilkins, 1985, pp 918–924

Benedek EP: Children and psychic trauma: a brief review of contemporary thinking, in Post-Traumatic Stress Disorder in Children. Edited by Eth S, Pynoos RS. Washington, DC, American Psychiatric Press, 1985, pp 1–16

Bloch D, Silber E, Perry S: Some factors in the emotional reactions of children to disaster. Am J Psychiatry 113:416–422, 1956

Burke JD Jr, Borus JF, Burns BJ, et al: Changes in children's behavior after a natural disaster. Am J Psychiatry 139:1010–1014, 1982

Carey-Trefzer CJ: The results of a clinical study of war-damaged children who attended the child guidance clinic, The Hospital for Sick Children, Great Ormond Street, London. Journal of Mental Science XCV:535–559, 1949

Daly RR: Samuel Pepys and posttraumatic stress disorder. Br J Psychiatry 143:64–68, 1983

Eth S, Pynoos RS (eds): Post-Traumatic Stress Disorder in Children. Washington, DC, American Psychiatric Press, 1985

Freud S: An infantile neurosis (1918), in The Standard Edition of the Complete Psychological Works of Sigmund Freud, Vol 17. Translated and edited by Strachey J. London, Hogarth Press, 1959, pp 7–122

Freud S: Inhibitions, symptoms and anxiety (1926), in The Standard Edition of the Complete Psychological Works of Sigmund Freud, Vol 20. Translated and edited by Strachey J. London, Hogarth Press, 1959, pp 75–175

Freud A, Burlingham D: War and Children. New York, Medical War Books, 1943

Gleser GC, Green BL, Winget C: Prolonged Psychosocial Effects of Disaster: A Study of Buffalo Creek. New York, Academic Press, 1981

Green BL: Evaluating the effects of disasters. Psychological Assessment 3:538–546, 1991

Green BL, Korol M, Grace MC, et al: Children and disaster: age, gender, and parental effects of PTSD symptoms. J Am Acad Child Adolesc Psychiatry 30:945–951, 1991

Helzer J, Robins L, McEvoy L: Post-traumatic stress disorder in the general population. N Engl J Med 317:1630–1634, 1987

Jones RT, Ribbie DP: Child, adolescent, and adult victims of residential fire: Psychosocial consequences. Behav Modif 15:560–580, 1991

Kinzie JD, Sack WH, Angell RH, et al: The psychiatric effects of massive trauma on Cambodian children; I: the children. Am Acad Child Adolesc Psychiatry 25:370–376, 1986

Kliman G: Psychological Emergencies of Childhood. New York, Grune & Stratton, 1968

Lacey G: Observations of Aberfan. J Psychosom Res 16:257–260, 1972

Levy DM: Psychic trauma of operations in children. Am J Dis Child 69:7–25, 1945

Lyons J: Post-traumatic stress disorder in children and adolescents. J Dev Behav Pediatr 8:349–356, 1987

March J: The nosology of post-traumatic stress disorder. Journal of Anxiety Disorders 4:61–82, 1990

Newman CJ: Children of disaster: clinical observations at Buffalo Creek. Am J Psychiatry 133:306–312, 1976

Pynoos RS: Post-traumatic stress disorder in children and adolescents, in Psychiatric Disorders in Children and Adolescents. Edited by Garfinkel BD, Carlson GA, Weller EB. Philadelphia, PA, WB Saunders, 1990, pp 48–63

Pynoos RS, Eth S: Children traumatized by witnessing acts of personal violence: homicide, rape, or suicide behavior, in Post-Traumatic Stress Disorder in Children. Edited by Eth S, Pynoos RS. Washington, DC, American Psychiatric Press, 1985, pp 17–43

Pynoos RS, Nader K: Children who witness the sexual assault of their mothers. Am Acad Child Adolesc Psychiatry 27:567–572, 1988

Pynoos RS, Frederick C, Nader K, et al: Life threat and post-traumatic stress in school-age children. Arch Gen Psychiatry 44:1057–1063, 1987

Pynoos RS, Nader K: Prevention of psychiatric morbidity in children after diaster, in Prevention of Mental Disorders, Alcohol, and Other Drug Use in Children and Adolescents. Washington, DC, U. S. Department of Health and Human Services, 1989, pp 225–271

Rhodes R: A Hole in the World. New York, Simon & Schuster, 1990

Rosenheck R, Nathan P: Secondary traumatization in the children of Vietnam veterans. Hosp Community Psychiatry 36:538–539, 1985

Russell DEH: The Secret Trauma: Incest in the Lives of Girls and Women. New York, Basic Books, 1986

Schwarz ED, Kowalski JM: Malignant memories: PTSD in children and adults after a school shooting. J Am Acad Child Adolesc Psychiatry 30:936–944, 1991

Shore J, Tatum E, Vollmer W: Psychiatric reactions to disaster: the Mt. St. Helen's Experience. Am J Psychiatry 143:590–595, 1986

Terr L: Children of Chowchilla. Psychoanal Study Child 34:547–623, 1979

Terr L: What happens to early memory of trauma? A study of twenty children under age five at the time of the documented traumatic events. J Am Acad Child Adolesc Psychiatry 27:96–104, 1988

Terr L: Too Scared to Cry. New York, Harper & Row, 1990

Vogel JM, Vernberg EM: Psychological Needs in Children in the Aftermath of Disasters: A Report of the Task Force on Children's Psychological Reactions to National and Human-Made Disasters. Washington, DC, American Psychiatric Association, 1992

Guidelines for the Forensic Psychological Assessment of Posttraumatic Stress Disorder Claimants

Terence M. Keane, Ph.D.

This chapter presents a multidimensional approach to the psychological assessment of posttraumatic stress disorder (PTSD), with a particular emphasis on reviewing the extant psychological tests, clinical interviews, and the data substantiating their use in the measurement of PTSD. Issues of etiology, causality, severity, and course generally are prominent in forensic examinations, but with respect to PTSD these factors assume increasing importance and salience. Procuring information and data that bear on each of these dimensions is a primary goal of the comprehensive assessment of PTSD recommended in this chapter. Accordingly, appropriate psychological assessment for PTSD involves a series of integrated steps for the clinician.

To obtain needed information on which the clinician can draw reliable and valid conclusions regarding the diagnosis of PTSD and its impact, the following steps are to be considered when possible:

1. The conduct of a standard comprehensive clinical examination that focuses on family and developmental history and preevent and postevent factors related to current day functioning; this examination would also include the procurement of information on the traumatic event itself in considerable detail

2. The use of a structured clinical interview that provides an opportunity to explore the range of possible Axis I and Axis II diagnoses that may be applicable to the individual (e.g., the Structured Clinical Interview for DSM-III-R [SCID; Spitzer et al. 1990])
3. The use of general personality questionnaires to provide information on functioning more broadly (e.g., the Minnesota Multiphasic Personality Inventory [MMPI; Hathaway and McKinley 1989])
4. The administering of specific tests that directly measure PTSD and its associated clinical features (e.g., the Mississippi PTSD Scale [Keane et al. 1988b])
5. The inclusion of measures of social role functioning to determine the extent of social and vocational impairment (e.g., Social Adjustment Scale [Weissman et al. 1990])

Clinical judgment is required when evaluating and integrating the data from all of these measures and in adjudicating information that is discrepant regarding the presence or absence of PTSD.

Since the inclusion of PTSD in the diagnostic nomenclature of the DSM-III (American Psychiatric Association 1980), research and development has centered on appropriate measurement strategies. In the intervening years there has been considerable progress in PTSD assessment, and these advances have been driven by conceptual models regarding the assessment of psychopathology generally and PTSD specifically (e.g., Keane et al. 1987; Sutker et al. 1991). These models have emphasized the importance of a comprehensive evaluation of 1) the nature of traumatic events (e.g., intensity, frequency, duration, detailed descriptors), 2) the characteristics of the person exposed (e.g., demographic data, personality factors, pretrauma vulnerabilities and strengths), and 3) the expression of symptoms by a person in certain ideographic patterns following exposure. The conceptual approaches advocated by clinicians to assessing PTSD are at once dynamic and interactive, placing a greater emphasis on longitudinal rather than cross-sectional views in understanding the many possible psychological outcomes associated with exposure to traumatic stressors. These conceptual models offer an excellent premise and foundation for the psychological assessment of PTSD in the forensic arena.

In addition to the conceptual models for assessing PTSD, Keane et al. (1987) also recommended that clinicians secure information from people other than the individual under examination and from as many sources as possible. The use of multiple methods of data collection within a measurement domain (e.g., psychological testing) was also recommended. Thus information from the informant, collateral sources (e.g., family, friends, neighbors, employees), structured clinical interviews, psychometric measures, and even psychophysiological assessment creates vectors of convergence from which the clinician can draw conclusions regarding the presence or absence of PTSD and its impact on social, marital, and vocational functioning. Given the imperfect nature of any single measure of PTSD, or of any psychological disorder for that matter, it is important for the clinician to apply this multidimensional approach to the assessment of PTSD.

Issues in the Psychological Assessment of PTSD

As stated previously in Chapter 2 of this book, the proper evaluation of PTSD contains many dimensions for the clinician to consider. Possibly the most frequent problem made by clinicians in conducting psychological assessments for PTSD is the assumption by the clinician that when a person is exposed to a stressor of traumatic proportions the psychological consequences are necessarily PTSD. The research literature clearly suggests that PTSD is only one of many possible consequences associated with trauma exposure (e.g., Keane and Wolfe 1990; Shore et al. 1986). Other disorders such as depression, generalized anxiety, substance abuse, and panic can also occur after traumatic exposure. As a result it is critical to determine the extent to which PTSD is present or absent in the subject examined.

A second feature of the PTSD examination is to ensure that PTSD, when it is observed, is secondary to the event in question. As our society enters an increasingly technological era, the possibilities for exposure to high-magnitude stressors over the course of the lifetime expand. Coupled with the dramatic rise in violence, and in particular sexual assault and domestic battering, there is a distinct possibility that a person can be exposed to multiple traumatic events. Some researchers have found that exposure to a traumatic event and the subsequent development of PTSD may indeed be related to previous trauma exposure (e.g., Helzer et al. 1987; Kilpatrick et al. 1992; Kulka et al. 1990). These research findings compel clinicians to examine patients for a range of traumatic events beyond the target event in litigation. Efforts to attribute psychological functioning to a single event will be significantly diminished if examinations by others indicate the presence of exposure to additional high-magnitude life events that could themselves yield PTSD. Assessment of social role functioning before and after the event in question is of paramount importance in understanding the role of the targeted event in the life of the person.

A third issue of some importance in PTSD assessment is the presence of a previously existing psychological disorder. Research to date indicates that one of the major vulnerabilities in the development of PTSD once an individual is exposed to a traumatic stressor is the existence of preexisting psychopathology (Helzer et al. 1987; Keane et al. 1993; Kulka et al. 1990). If preexisting psychopathology is evident, then the clinician's attention should address issues of severity of disorder by virtue of the addition of the PTSD comorbidity. Moreover, deterioration in psychosocial functioning that may be apparent in the interpersonal, social, marital, parental, or, most important, the vocational domain would then assume increased importance. Identification of changes in functioning concurrent with the traumatic exposure is generally key in circumstances of litigation but is crucial when a psychiatric history is present. Moreover, the addition of a concurrent disorder (in this case, PTSD) to the preexisting condition unquestionably leads to a more severe psychological condition, and this would be reflected most aptly in clinician ratings on Axis IV (i.e., psychosocial stressors' severity) and Axis V (i.e., global assessment of functioning). Such information would be clearly relevant to the forensic case at hand.

A fourth issue associated with the assessment of PTSD is the frequent association of PTSD with other Axis I disorders. Even in cases in which there is no previous psychological disorder, the presence of PTSD is often complicated by the emergence of other disorders concurrently or over time. In particular, disorders such as major depression and substance abuse can obfuscate the clinical picture and confuse even the most discerning eye. With respect to major depression, the clinician is most often struck by the unremitting course of the disorder since the occurrence of the traumatic event. Unlike other forms of depression seen in the absence of PTSD, depression, when combined with PTSD, seems to remain relatively constant—and sometimes in the most nefarious cases it is even exacerbated over time. Phenomenologically, the depressive state appears more as a "double depression," bearing characteristics of both major depression and dysthymia.

If substance abuse is involved, it is important to clarify the onset of the alcohol or drug use. Most often in cases of trauma, the substance abuse is an effort to self-medicate the anxiety, depression, and emotional numbing of PTSD (Keane et al. 1988a). This pattern obviously contributes to the complexity of the case as the substance abuse, seen as secondary to the development of PTSD, contributes to the downward spiral in multidimensional life functioning.

Attention to each of these issues can prevent problems for the clinician as litigation proceeds. A comprehensive history, noting onset of problems and their phenomenological course, can promote optimal understanding of the person being evaluated and the legitimacy of his or her claim and case. Failure to appreciate the interrelationship of the disorders and issues highlighted above can mitigate the cogency of the arguments proffered by the clinician and lawyer.

Psychological Assessment of PTSD

The purpose of this section is to provide empirical information regarding psychometric characteristics of structured clinical interviews that have been developed for the measurement of PTSD and psychological tests that have been especially developed for assessing PTSD. Each of the assessment instruments included in this section has been selected on the basis of substantive research, and although the list included here is not exhaustive, it provides an excellent starting point for clinicians who are interested in evaluating clients for the presence of PTSD.

Structured Interviews

The SCID (Spitzer et al. 1990) is the interview most frequently employed to date in the evaluation of PTSD. The SCID provides a comprehensive evaluation of all Axis I and Axis II psychiatric diagnoses. The PTSD module is concise, it is relatively easy to administer and score, and it addresses the major diagnostic features of the disorder. Kulka et al. (1990), in their study of Vietnam War veterans, found that the SCID had a kappa interrater reliability score of .93 when a second clinician listened to audiotapes of the target interview and then made independent diagnoses. McFall et al. (1990) reported 100% diagnostic reliability between two clinicians who completed independent SCIDs on 10 subjects. Keane et al. (1988c) observed a kappa of .68 for PTSD SCID diagnoses derived from two independent clinicians who individually interviewed the same patients ($N = 39$). Kulka et al. (1990) also found the SCID diagnosis to be strongly correlated with other psychometrically sound indices of PTSD (i.e., Mississippi Scale, Impact of Event Scale, and Keane PTSD Scale of the MMPI). These results suggest that the PTSD module of the SCID is a measure with respectable reliability and validity. The instrument does, however, have limitations. The SCID yields only dichotomous information about the presence or absence of each of the symptom criteria for the disorder. Consequently, measures of disorder severity and changes in symptom level over time cannot be easily detected using the SCID. Yet this instrument is clearly the most widely used measure for evaluating PTSD and accompanying disorders and has significant value in terms of its structured nature in guiding a clinician's evaluation for PTSD.

The Diagnostic Interview Scale (DIS-NIMH; Robins et al. 1981) is a highly structured interview that can be administered by either technicians or clinicians. Providing a comprehensive examination of the diagnostic categories, this instrument has been used in many epidemiological studies across the world. In a review of the literature on PTSD assessment, Watson et al. (1991) noted that in clinical settings, the PTSD-DIS functioned well, correlating highly with other known measures of PTSD. However, Kulka et al. (1991) indicated that when used with a community sample in which the base rate of PTSD was low, the DIS performed poorly, with estimates of .23 for sensitivity (i.e., the proportion of true cases identified by the test) and .28 for kappa (i.e., the proportion of agreement above chance levels). The use of this highly structured instrument for making diagnoses in field studies has, therefore, been challenged, and additional work is needed to substantiate its utility in those settings. Data on its use in clinical settings seem to more strongly support its usefulness. As a structured interview, the DIS also suffers from the same limitation as the SCID in that the presence or absence of a particular symptom is rated dichotomously. This, then, reduces the capacity of the clinician to distinguish symptom and disorder severity.

The PTSD Interview (Watson et al. 1991) yields both dichotomous and continuous scores, thus addressing some of the limitations of the SCID and DIS-NIMH. Reports of high test/retest reliability (.95), internal stability (α = .92; i.e., a test's internal reliability), sensitivity (.89; i.e., the proportion of true cases correctly identified by a test), specificity (.94; i.e., the proportion of noncases correctly identified by a test), and kappa (.82) recommend this instrument for use in diagnosing PTSD. This instrument differs, however, from other clinical instruments in that it asks the subjects to make their own rating of symptom severity rather than requiring this task of the clinician. This self-rating minimizes the role of the experienced clinician in the diagnostic process. It also minimizes the experience that the clinician has in comparing symptom severity from one case of PTSD to others that he or she may have seen in clinical practice.

Davidson et al. (1990) offer the Structured Interview for PTSD (SI-PTSD) as an alternative to the SCID and DIS. This instrument also contains continuous and dichotomous symptom ratings, and the researchers have found that it is a psychometrically sound instrument. Measures of excellent test/retest reliability (.71), interrater reliability (.97–.99), and perfect diagnostic agreement ($N = 34$) were reported in the preliminary article by Davidson and colleagues. More comprehensive utility analyses revealed a sensitivity of .96, a specificity of .80, and a kappa of .79 when compared with diagnoses by clinicians using the SCID. Clearly, this instrument has major advantages for use in the clinic setting and is an excellent prototype for use when making PTSD diagnoses in the forensic setting.

The Clinician-Administered PTSD Scale (CAPS; Blake et al. 1991) was developed to address the limitations of previous clinical interviews for assessing PTSD. Available in both a lifetime and current version, the CAPS contains diagnostic symptoms of PTSD, the associated features of PTSD, symptom severity measures, indices of impairment in social and occupational functioning, and an assessment of validity and degree of confidence by the clinician in the patient's responses. The CAPS also provides continuous and dichotomous scores to suit the needs of the clinician or the research investigator. Preliminary results from a sophisticated psychometric assessment of its properties (Weathers 1992) indicate that the CAPS is promising with respect to issues of diagnostic reliability and validity as well as with regard to measures of sensitivity, specificity, and kappa. Perhaps the major advantage of the CAPS in a forensic setting is that it not only requires the clinician to evaluate the presence and severity of various symptoms associated with PTSD but also provides an opportunity for the clinician to evaluate the impact of the symptoms on an individual's social and vocational function. Impact on these domains is a key determinant of damages by plaintiffs in civil litigation suits.

Psychometric Measures

Numerous questionnaires and self-report measures of PTSD have been developed and enjoy widespread use in clinical, research, and forensic settings. Each measure has diagnostic utility as well as the capacity to assess the severity of the disorder. The major advantage of the use of psychometric measures is that the clinician can compare scores on these measures of PTSD for the person being evaluated against hundreds and sometimes even thousands of people on whom the norms for these questionnaires have been based. Each of the measures described below has diagnostic utility and, because these measures are relatively inexpensive to employ, several are frequently administered in conjunction with the clinical interview to provide multiple indices of PTSD. As mentioned in the introductory section, no single measure of PTSD is perfectly reliable and valid; therefore, the use of multiple measures is important to the clinician to ensure that the conclusions made clinically are supported by data obtained from multiple methods of study.

The Keane PTSD Scale of the MMPI (Keane et al. 1984) consists of 49 items from the 399 Form-R version of the MMPI. These 49 items were found to differentiate a PTSD sample from non-PTSD patients in both a test sample and a cross-validation sample of veterans. Eight-two percent of 200 subjects were correctly classified using a cutoff score of 30. Subsequent studies have not found the same diagnostic hit rate, a problem that might be due to varying base rates of PTSD in the sample under study, different diagnostic methods for arriving at cases and noncases, or the overreliance on a single cutoff score to make the diagnosis. In a study of forensic cases, Koretsky and Peck (1990) found that a cutoff score of 20 or above was strongly correlated with a diagnosis of PTSD among people who were exposed to life-and-death situations, such as train crashes, car wrecks, and industrial accidents. Because few studies have been conducted on this measure with multiple trauma categories, it is impossible to arrive at one single cutoff score that may reflect PTSD. Rather, the clinician is encouraged to consider the PTSD scale of the MMPI as a continuous measure of "PTSD-ness," indicating the extent and severity of PTSD, rather than serving as a rigid, dichotomous measure of PTSD.

With the publication of the MMPI-2, Lyons and Keane (1992) described the use of the Keane PTSD Scale within the context of the improved overall instrument. For the most part, the scale remains unchanged in terms of the specific wording of items; however, three repeated items have been deleted, as were all repeated items on the test. The performance of the PTSD Scale in the National Vietnam Veterans Readjustment Study (NVVRS) (Kulka et al. 1990) indicates that the MMPI-2 modifications have not altered the general interrelationship of the Keane PTSD Scale with other measures of PTSD.

The Mississippi PTSD Scale (Keane et al. 1988b) is available in both civilian and combat versions. It is a 35-item instrument that has high internal consistency ($\alpha = .94$), test/retest reliability (.97), sensitivity (.93), and specificity (.89). This instrument performed effectively in both clinical settings (e.g., McFall et al. 1990) and in field settings (e.g., Kulka et al. 1990), an unusual finding for any psychological test. These results indicate general utility for measuring PTSD across settings and for different purposes. The Mississippi PTSD Scale measures the diagnostic criteria from the DSM as well as the associated features of PTSD. It is self-administered by the patient, and its scoring and interpretation are relatively straightforward. Numerous research studies from different laboratories have concluded that the Mississippi PTSD Scale is an excellent instrument for assessing PTSD across clinical and research settings (Keane et al. 1988b; McFall et al. 1990; Watson 1990).

The Impact of Event Scale (IES; Horowitz et al. 1979) focuses on the assessment of the intrusions and avoidance or numbing symptoms of PTSD. Designed prior to the inclusion of PTSD in the DSM-III, the IES does not contain a comprehensive evaluation of PTSD and its associative features. Despite this limitation, the IES is perhaps the single most widely used instrument for assessing the psychological consequences of traumatic events. Not surprisingly, studies have found that the IES is correlated with other diagnostic measures of PTSD even though the IES does not contain all of the symptoms associated with PTSD. These findings are indicative of the central importance of the intrusive or reliving symptoms and the avoidance/numbing symptoms in the PTSD diagnosis. The IES has been found to have strong internal consistency (.78 for intrusion; .82 for avoidance) and test/retest reliability (.89 for intrusion; .79 for avoidance). Used in conjunction with other, more comprehensive measures of PTSD, the IES is an excellent choice for evaluating the subjective distress related to a specific stressful event in a person's life.

Saunders et al. (1990) derived a 28-item PTSD scale for the Symptom Checklist—90 (SCL-90; Derogatis 1983) using items that best discriminated women with crime-related PTSD from those who did not have PTSD. With good sensitivity (.75) and high specificity (.90) using the DIS-NIMH as the criterion, this instrument can be a particularly valuable addition to the psychological battery of the clinician. The SCL-90 is a widely used psychological test that evaluates the presence, absence, and severity of a wide range of psychological symptoms that can be associated with traumatic stressors. Although this PTSD scale needs cross-validation and replication, the possibility of employing a subsection of the SCL-90 to measure PTSD would be a welcome addition to the psychological test armamentarium of the clinician.

The Penn Inventory for PTSD (Hammerberg 1992) is an important new diagnostic tool for the measurement of PTSD because it was developed and validated with both combat veterans and trauma-exposed, nonveteran samples. This particular instrument has internal consistency ($\alpha = .94$) and high test/retest reliability (.96). Sensitivity was .90 and specificity was 100% among a sample of 83 veterans; in a sample of disaster survivors, sensitivity was 94%, with specificity observed to be 100% for the PTSD diagnosis. Although these findings are with relatively small numbers of subjects, it is clear that the Penn Inventory for PTSD has excellent potential as a questionnaire measure of PTSD symptomatology. Further research studies documenting its overall utility in a variety of settings would be welcome. Its major advantages are that it is easy to use, straightforward to administer, and it already contains norms on both combat and civilian populations.

Psychophysiological Studies of PTSD

The search for biological measures of a psychological disorder transcends the study of PTSD and has been the focus of considerable interest of psychobiologists and biological psychiatrists. Early work in the area of PTSD indicated that a psychological challenge (i.e., exposure to cues of a traumatic event) can provoke systematic physiological responses across several measurement domains (e.g., heart rate, skin conductance, EMG, blood pressure). Blanchard et al. (1982) and Malloy et al. (1983) found that this reactivity predicted the PTSD diagnosis when using auditory and audiovisual cues to stimulate reactivity. Some years later, Pitman et al. (1987) observed the same reactivity using personal scripts of traumatic events that were then read to subjects. These studies all observed robust physiological reactivity when combining the presentation of a psychologically meaningful cue and concurrently measuring psychophysiological responses. This challenge model for assessing PTSD may help us identify other psychophysiological parameters associated with this disorder. With respect to forensic cases, the use of ideographic cues stemming from the traumatic incidents while concomitantly measuring psychophysiological reactivity may provide measures of PTSD other than self-report. In addition, the psychophysiological reactivity can provide important biological information regarding the actual physiological effects of an assault, an accident, or another form of disaster.

With ongoing large-scale physiological studies soon to be completed (Keane et al. 1988c), the potential value of these physiological markers for PTSD will be available in the very near future. To date, the data from several other research laboratories do, indeed, indicate that there is a strong physiological component associated with the diagnosis of PTSD. These findings, if replicated in larger scale studies, would provide important new information for use in forensic cases. Pitman et al. (1994) have recommended the use of psychophysiological measures to verify the presence of one dimension of the disorder, reactivity to cues reminiscent of the trauma, and as a measure of the presence of PTSD. Using psychophysiological procedures for the former has been universally acceptable to courts. The latter use remains an open empirical question. However, it is important to consider that physiological reactivity to cues reminiscent of the traumatic event remains only one data point in the complex algorithm of psychological tests, structured interviews, and clinical interviews conducted by the clinician. All tests bear some imperfection, and differences in the vectors for PTSD must always be reconciled through clinical judgment. This judgment is best informed through the comprehensive history, a complete review of the medical records, and a thorough understanding of the circumstances surrounding the traumatic event and the person's role in that event.

As is readily observed by the results of this review on the psychological assessment of PTSD, progress in this arena has been rapid since the inclusion of this diagnosis in the DSM-III in 1980. Clinicians and researchers are now in an excellent position to conduct meaningful evaluations of their patients. Evaluations that include information from structured interviews and psychological tests can be informed by any of a number of outstanding instruments developed specifically to measure PTSD, its associated features, and the impact of these symptoms on multidimensional life functioning. Although PTSD is a disorder with a short history in the diagnostic manual, the measures of PTSD rival those now available for assessing major depression, schizophrenia, the anxiety disorders, and the personality disorders. Indeed, the appropriate assessment of PTSD now should include one or more of these standardized and validated instruments for use in forensic settings. These instruments can readily inform the clinician about the status of PTSD in an individual client compared with others with similar exposure and symptom complaints.

The Forensic Psychological Report

Perhaps the most critical piece of the forensic psychological examination is the report. Therein, the clinician records the nature and purpose of the examination and integrates the data obtained from all sources. Most important is the conceptual formulation of the case and its bearing on the legal points in question. Whether the report is written 1) for the defendant in an insanity plea in a criminal case, 2) for a plaintiff to describe the consequences of criminal victimization, or 3) for the plaintiff in a civil suit documenting damages, the report should contain coverage of specific topics. Table 5–1 contains an example of the format to be used in completing a forensic psychological report. Each section of the report is explained in the following discussion.

Referral Source and Referral Questions

Contained in this section is the purpose for which the clinician conducted the examination and assessment. In addition, the source of the referral should be specified in the report, whether it be another health care professional, a lawyer, or a self-referral.

Limits of Confidentiality

Reports written for forensic purposes are usually disseminated to the lawyers involved in the case, the court, jury members, and other health care professionals involved in the case. These limits on confidentiality should be explained to the client in clear language. An estimate of his or her comprehension of these limits should be included in the body of the report.

Table 5–1. Template for use in preparing a report for forensic psychological examination

---

Forensic Psychological Report
1. Referral source and referral questions
2. Limits of confidentiality
3. Review of records (list and document):
   - ❑ Medical
   - ❑ Legal/police
   - ❑ Psychological
   - ❑ Social/vocational
4. Methods of assessment (list, date, duration):
   - ❑ Relevant history
   - ❑ Mental status examination
   - ❑ Structured interview
   - ❑ Psychological tests
   - ❑ Neuropsychological tests
   - ❑ Physiological tests (e.g., CAT, MRI, psychophysiological exams)
5. Results of examination and special test
6. Collateral reports (relationship, dates of inquiry)
7. Forensic case formulation
8. Diagnostic formulation/multiaxial classification

Review of Records

All records reviewed by the clinician that influenced the opinion on the case should be listed in the text of the report. Such records could include but are not necessarily limited to the following: 1) medical records, 2) legal records, 3) police documents, 4) psychological records and reports, and 5) social and vocational records that can assist the clinician in documenting pre- and postevent functioning. The records should be listed by date and name so that they can be readily identified by the reader. These records can detail the event, and in the case of a public disaster, media reports can be included from printed or televised sources.

Methods of Assessment

To provide the reader with an understanding of the nature and extent of the psychological examination conducted by the clinician, this section should include a listing of the many methods employed by the clinician to arrive at the opinion in the case. Interviews, their dates of occurrence, and their duration provide an in-depth understanding of the opportunities for sampling the examinee's behavior across settings and time. The greater the diversity and number of interviews, the larger the sample of behavior and, thereby, the more reliable the findings. If specialized tests are employed, these should be incorporated into this section of the report, and if the examiner ordered but did not conduct these tests him- or herself, the responsible or administering clinician as well as the location of the testing laboratory should be identified.

Results of Examination and Special Test

This section of the report should incorporate the precise results obtained from the clinical interview, the structured interview, the psychological tests, and the physiological tests if any were employed. The groundwork for the expert opinion is laid in this section of the report, and, correspondingly, considerable attention to detail and accuracy is required. The interrelationship of the various measures of PTSD and social functioning should be highlighted and the conceptual integration of results provided. Also in this section, the clinician provides relevant demographic, family, marital, and developmental information as it pertains to the issue in question. Previously existing psychological conditions or vulnerabilities should be identified here so that a more complete understanding of the examinee is possible in view of the legal question under scrutiny. A special section of the results should be dedicated to explicating the findings from the mental status examination.

Collateral Reports

When it is possible and valuable to obtain information from collateral sources (e.g., family members, friends, neighbors, employees) for purposes of documenting a decline in social or vocational functioning or for verifying symptom complaints, then a listing of these interviews with results should be included in the report. These data are particularly useful in documenting changes in social or vocational functioning concomitant with the traumatic event per se.

Forensic Case Formulation

In this section, data from all sources are integrated into a conceptual framework from which statements can be made regarding the specific legal standards that are relevant to the case. Avoiding psychological jargon whenever possible, the examiner provides the most sophisticated conceptual analysis possible given the extant data. The basis for the expert opinion should be clearly presented and all relevant information organized in such a way that it is understandable to other health professionals, lawyers, the court, and, if relevant, the jury. Questions of damages, causation, and sanity when involved should be clearly stated in this section, and the opinion should be stated unmistakably, using language that meets the pertinent legal standard involved.

Diagnostic Formulation/ Multiaxial Classification

The DSM-III, DSM-III-R (American Psychiatric Association 1987), and DSM-IV (American Psychiatric Association 1994) all employ a multiaxial classification scheme. The final section of the report should include diagnostic formulations for Axes I–V. A report including only Axis I and II is necessarily incomplete, and all reports should contain information for all five axes, even if the opinion on a particular axis is deferred for insufficient information. Some individuals will meet criteria for multiple psychiatric diagnoses, and they can be listed on Axis I or II. The primary diagnosis of relevance to the case can, accordingly, be listed first within an axis if there are multiple comorbid diagnoses on the same axis (e.g., PTSD and substance abuse).

Summary

Forensic psychological examinations can be of unique value to the court in deciding the outcome of a variety of complex cases involving PTSD. The current availability of excellent structured interviews for PTSD and a number of psychological tests expressly developed for assessing the presence and the severity of PTSD lends increased credibility in the courtroom to the clinician who chooses to use these contemporary methods.

Data on the presence or absence of any psychiatric disorder are usually based on self-report and thus warrant some skepticism in courtroom situations. The opinion of the informed clinician who relies on the use of multiple sources of information over time, who uses collateral informants, who assiduously peruses all pertinent records, and who employs psychological, neuropsychological, and physiological tests with sound psychometric properties merits the attention of all those involved in the case and minimizes the skepticism often associated with less thorough and competent psychological assessment. The use of these more contemporary methods in conjunction with a skillful and intuitive clinical examination is the hallmark of an outstanding psychological examination.

References

American Psychiatric Association: Diagnostic and Statistical Manual of Mental Disorders, 3rd Edition. Washington, DC, American Psychiatric Association, 1980

American Psychiatric Association: Diagnostic and Statistical Manual of Mental Disorders, 3rd Edition, Revised. Washington, DC, American Psychiatric Association, 1987

American Psychiatric Association: Diagnostic and Statistical Manual of Mental Disorders, 4th Edition. Washington, DC, American Psychiatric Association, 1994

Blake DD, Weathers FW, Nagy LN, et al: A clinician rating scale for assessing current and lifetime PTSD: the CAPS-1. Behavior Therapist 18:187–188, 1990

Blanchard EB, Kolb LC, Pallmeyer TP, et al: A psychophysiological study of posttraumatic stress disorder in Vietnam veterans. Psychiatr Q 54:220–229, 1982

Davidson J, Kudler H, Smith R: Treatment of posttraumatic stress disorder. Am J Psychiatry 47:259–266, 1990

Hammerberg M: Penn Inventory for posttraumatic stress disorder: psychometric properties. Psychological Assessment 4:67–76, 1992

Hathaway SR, McKinley JC: Minnesota Multiphasic Personality Inventory—2. Minneapolis, MN, University of Minnesota, 1989

Helzer JE, Robins LN, McEvoy L: Post-traumatic stress disorder in the general population: findings of the Epidemiologic Catchment Area survey. N Engl J Med 317:1630–1634, 1987

Horowitz MJ, Wilner NR, Alvarez W: Impact of Event Scale: a measure of subject stress. Psychosom Med 41:209–218, 1979

Keane TM, Wolfe J: Co-morbidity in post-traumatic stress disorder: an analysis of community and clinical studies. Journal of Applied Social Psychology 20:1776–1788, 1990

Keane TM, Malloy PF, Fairbank JA: Empirical development of an MMPI subscale for the assessment of combat-related post-traumatic stress disorder. J Consult Clin Psychol 5:888–891, 1984

Keane TM, Wolfe J, Taylor KL: Post-traumatic stress disorder: evidence for diagnostic validity and methods of psychological assessment. J Clin Psychol 43:32–43, 1987

Keane TM, Gerardi RJ, Lyons JA, et al: The interrelationship of substance abuse and PTSD: epidemiological and clinical considerations, in Recent Developments in Alcoholism, Vol 6. Edited by Galanter M. New York, Plenum, 1988a

Keane TM, Caddell JM, Taylor KL: Mississippi Scale for Combat-Related Posttraumatic Stress Disorder: three studies in reliability and validity. J Consult Clin Psychol 56:85–90, 1988b

Keane TM, Kolb L, Thomas RT: A Psychophysiological Study of Chronic PTSD. Cooperative Study #334. Vol I, October, 1988c

Keane TM, Zimering RT, Knight JA, et al: Post-traumatic stress disorder, in Psychopathology in Adulthood: An Advanced Text. Edited by Bellack A, Hersen M. Needham, MA, Allyn and Bacon, 1993

Kilpatrick DG, Edmunds CN, Seymour AK: Rape in America: A Report to the Nation. Arlington, VA, National Victims Center, 1992

Koretsky MB, Peck AH: Validation and cross-validation of the PTSD scale of the MMPI with civilian trauma victims. J Clin Psychol 46:296–300, 1990

Kulka RA, Schlenger WE, Fairbank JA, et al: Trauma and the Vietnam War Generation. New York, Brunner/Mazel, 1990

Lyons JA, Keane TM: Keane PTSD scale: MMPI and MMPI-2 update. Journal of Traumatic Stress 5:111–117, 1992

Malloy PF, Fairbank JA, Keane TM: Validation of a multimethod assessment of posttraumatic stress disorders in Vietnam veterans. J Consult Clin Psychol 51:488–494, 1983

McFall ME, Smith DE, Mackay PW, et al: Reliability and validity of Mississippi Scale for combat-related posttraumatic stress disorder. Psychological Assessment 2:114–121, 1990

Pitman RK, Orr SP, Forgue DF, et al: Psychophysiologic assessment of posttraumatic stress disorder imagery in Vietnam combat veterans. Arch Gen Psychiatry 44:970–975, 1987

Pitman RK, Saunders LS, Orr SP: Psychophysiologic testing for post-traumatic stress disorder. Trial, April 1994, pp 22–26

Robins L, Helzer J, Croughan J, et al: NIMH–Diagnostic Interview Schedule: its history, characteristics, and validity. Arch Gen Psychiatry 38:381–389, 1981

Saunders BE, Arata CM, Kilpatrick DG: Development of a crime-related post-traumatic stress disorder scale for women within the Symptom Checklist-90— Revised. Journal of Traumatic Stress 3:439–448, 1990

Shore JH, Tatum EL, Vollmer WM: Psychiatric reactions to disaster: the Mount St. Helens experience. Am J Psychiatry 143:590–595, 1986

Spitzer RL, Williams JBW, Gibbon M, et al: Structured Clinical Interview for DSM-III-R. Washington, DC, American Psychiatric Press, 1990

Sutker PB, Uddo-Crane M, Allain AN: Clinical and research assessment of posttraumatic stress disorder: a conceptual overview. Psychological Assessment 3:520–530, 1991

Watson CG: Psychometric posttraumatic stress disorder measurement techniques: a review. Psychological Assessment 2:460–469, 1990

Weathers FW: A psychometric analysis of the Clinicians Administered PTSD Scale. Department of Veterans Affairs Medical Research Service Research Advisory Grant, 1992

Weissman MS, Paykel ES, Prusoff BA: Social Adjustment Scale Handbook: Rationale, Reliability, Validity, Scoring, and Training Guide. New York, College of Physicians and Surgeons of Columbia University, 1990

Chapter 6

Guidelines for the Evaluation of Malingering in Posttraumatic Stress Disorder

Phillip J. Resnick, M.D.

The clinician who in a legal context evaluates a claimant for posttraumatic stress disorder (PTSD) must consider the possibility of malingering. Separate small clues that would lead to a more detailed investigation may otherwise be overlooked. The diagnosis of PTSD is based almost entirely on the claimant's report of subjective symptoms. The accessibility of specific DSM-IV (American Psychiatric Association 1994) criteria permits the resourceful malingerer to easily report the "right" symptoms. Hiding or minimizing symptoms, which are not addressed in this chapter, should be kept in mind by the clinician, especially in shame-sensitive persons.

Few personal injury cases reach the courts without an expressed or implied allegation of malingering (Lipman 1962). Suspicions of malingering help to explain why damages awarded for PTSD are substantially less than those for physical injury, despite the fact that limitations on the claimant's life may actually be greater (Trimble 1981).

The primary motivation to malinger PTSD is financial gain. It is the rare person who is not influenced to some degree by the possibility that an injury may lead to financial benefit (Keiser 1968). Schafer (1986) believes

Some portions of this chapter were modified with permission from "Malingering of Posttraumatic Disorders," in *Clinical Assessment of Malingering and Deception*. Edited by Rogers R. New York, Guilford, 1988, pp. 84–103.

that having a compensable injury promotes a "little larceny" in most litigants. In addition to financial compensation, sympathy and social support may be consciously sought by malingerers (Keiser 1968).

The concept of traumatic neuroses first arose from the belief that an accidental concussion to the spine caused abnormalities of the sympathetic nervous system (Clevenger 1889). The disorder was quickly seized upon by dishonest litigants seeking compensation after accidents (Hamilton 1906). PTSD has been given many labels since 1889, many of which suggest malingering (see Table 6–1). The introduction of PTSD as an official diagnosis in DSM-III (American Psychiatric Association 1980) caused a sharp increase in clinicians' sensitivity to this disorder and heightened concern about potential malingering.

Definitions

Malingering is listed in DSM-IV as a condition not attributable to a mental disorder. It is defined as the "intentional production of false or grossly exaggerated physical or psychological symptoms, motivated by external in-

---

Table 6–1.   Names used to describe posttraumatic stress disorder

Accident neurosis	Postaccident anxiety syndrome
Accident victim syndrome	Postaccident syndrome
Aftermath neurosis	Posttraumatic syndrome
American disease	Profit neurosis
Attitudinal pathosis	Railway spine
Compensation hysteria	Rape trauma syndrome
Compensationitis	Secondary gain neurosis
Compensation neurosis	Traumatic hysteria
Fright neurosis	Traumatic neurasthenia
Greenback neurosis	Traumatic neurosis
Justice neurosis	Triggered neurosis
Litigation neurosis	Unconscious malingering
Mediterranean back	Vertebral neurosis
Neurotic neurosis	Whiplash neurosis

Source.   Adapted from Mendelson 1984.

centives such as . . . financial compensation" (American Psychiatric Association 1994, p. 683). In contrast, a *factitious disorder* involves the intentional production of symptoms due to the internal motivation to assume a patient role. Both disorders require a deceitful state of mind.

Several other terms are useful in the description of malingering phenomena. *Pure malingering* is the feigning of disease when it does not exist at all. *Partial malingering* is the conscious exaggeration of existing symptoms or the fraudulent allegation that prior genuine symptoms are still present. In addition, the term *false imputation* refers to ascribing actual symptoms to a cause consciously recognized as having no relationship to the symptoms. For example, authentic psychiatric symptoms due to clearly defined stresses at home may be falsely attributed to a traumatic event at work in order to gain compensation.

Incidence

The incidence of malingered psychiatric symptoms after injury is unknown. Estimates vary from 1% (Keiser 1968) to over 50% (Henderson 1986; Miller and Cartlidge 1972), depending on whether those providing the information work for insurance companies or plaintiffs' attorneys. The frequency of the diagnosis varies with the astuteness and skepticism of the clinician. The U.S. General Accounting Office did a follow-up study on persons considered 100% disabled. Approximately 40% of those studied showed *no* disability whatsoever 1 year after their disability determinations (M. T. Maloney et al., unpublished observations, 1980). Pure malingering is uncommon in PTSD cases, but exaggeration of symptoms is quite common (Jones and Llewellyn 1917; Trimble 1981).

Reluctance to Diagnose Malingering

Even though court testimony about malingering is protected by immunity, concern over legal liability is a major reason for clinicians' hesitancy to label someone a malingerer (RESTATEMENT OF TORTS 1938). Most authors conservatively suggest that the clinician should only state that there is no objective evidence to support the claimant's subjective complaints (e.g., Davidson 1950). The possibility of provoking a physical assault by calling a person a malingerer is another source of concern (Hofling 1965).

Hurst (1940) suggested that there are only two situations in which a diagnosis of malingering can be confirmed with certainty: 1) when malingerers think they are unobserved and are caught in the act, and 2) when malingerers actually confess that they are faking. Unless the clinician has substantial evidence, it is usually best to state that it is not possible to reach a firm conclusion. When clear evidence is present, however, the diagnosis of malingering should be made.

Guidelines For Evaluation

Guidelines for the evaluation of malingering in claimants reporting symptoms of PTSD address 1) collateral data, 2) information obtained from the claimant, 3) the clinician's interview style in examining the claimant, 4) assessment of the differential diagnosis of malingered PTSD, and 5) threshold for a full assessment of malingering. Special guidelines for assessing PTSD in Vietnam War veterans are also proposed.

Guidelines for Collateral Data

Collateral information should include police reports about the traumatic incident, witness statements, and any past psychiatric records of the claimant. The examiner should interview at least one family member or close associate of the claimant—preferably in person but at least by telephone.

A thorough collection of collateral data is critical because of the subjective nature of PTSD symptoms. Complete progress notes of therapists, rather than summary letters, should always be reviewed. If the clinician possesses more factual information about the case than the claimant believes, it helps the examiner to assess the claimant's veracity. Records should be carefully reviewed before the clinical examination so that the claimant can be confronted with any contradictions between his or her history and the records.

Interviewing a family member, such as a spouse, provides valuable information to corroborate or contradict the claimant's version of his or her symptoms. The assertion that a claimant dreams or thinks about a traumatic event should be verified by relatives who have heard him or her talk about it in situations that are not related to the litigation. Such issues as the claimant's body movements during dreams, patterns of sleep, and changes in sexual interest can also be addressed.

Guidelines for Information Obtained From the Claimant

The clinician should take a detailed history of the traumatic event itself, the claimant's psychiatric symptoms, treatment efforts, and living patterns. The clinician should inquire about whether the claimant has filed any prior lawsuits or had any arrests for criminal charges.

In assessing malingering, it is useful to know whether the claimant is familiar with the diagnostic criteria for PTSD. The clinician should inquire about whether the claimant saw the trauma coming. Persons who feel helpless while anticipating a traumatic event are more likely to develop PTSD symptoms. The clinician should also inquire about the details of traumatic dreams and the capacity of the claimant to be able to work and enjoy recreation.

The clinician should obtain a detailed history of the claimant's living patterns preceding the stressor. Symptoms such as difficulty concentrating or insomnia may have been present before the traumatic event. Baseline activity in a typical week before the stressor should be compared with reported impairment at the time of the evaluation.

Guidelines for the Clinician's Interview Style in Examining the Claimant

While taking the history, the clinician should not communicate any bias or give any clues about how genuine PTSD manifests itself. Collateral informants should be seen separately from the claimant.

If the clinician begins the evaluation in a challenging manner, it may cause claimants to think that they must exaggerate their symptoms in order to be believed. The examiner should be particularly careful to ask open-ended questions and let claimants tell their complete stories with few interruptions. Details can be clarified with specific questions later.

Third parties should be excluded from the clinical evaluation of the claimant for two important reasons. First, the presence of relatives precludes using them to verify the accuracy of symptoms. Second, should the clinician wish to gently confront the claimant with the possibility of malingering, the absence of a third party will reduce loss of face.

Guidelines for Assessing the Differential Diagnosis of Malingered PTSD

In deciding whether symptoms of PTSD are malingered, the clinician should have a good understanding of the phenomenology of genuine PTSD. The clinician must carefully examine the appropriateness of the relationship between the symptoms and the stressor, the time elapsed between the stressor and symptom development, and the relationship between any prior psychiatric symptoms and current impairment.

Psychiatric disorders that occur after trauma include PTSD, malingering, depressive disorders, anxiety disorders, conversion disorders, postconcussion syndromes, and, psychoses. In cases of PTSD that follow accidents, the clinical picture may be complicated by physical symptoms, pain, and the sequelae of concussion. Some malingered claims of psychic damages originate after claims for physical injury are unsuccessful (Henderson 1986).

PTSD is often seen after vehicular accidents that cause head injury and concussion. *Postconcussive syndrome* is manifested by headaches, increased anxiety, emotional lability, concentration deficits, and memory problems (Lishman 1978). Even without loss of consciousness, head injuries may cause symptoms that can be easily confused with PTSD (Trimble 1981).

Malingerers may overact their part by describing PTSD symptoms in a dramatic manner. All malingerers are actors who portray their illness as they understand it (Ossipov 1944). They are more eager to call attention to their symptoms than are persons with genuine PTSD. Malingerers may seem evasive during the interview and be unwilling to make definite statements about returning to work or anticipation of financial gain.

A person who has always been a responsible and honest member of society is less likely to malinger PTSD (Davidson 1965). Malingerers are more likely to be marginal members of society with few binding ties or committed, long-standing financial responsibilities, such as home ownership (Braverman 1978). The malingerer may have a history of spotty employment, previous incapacitating injuries, and extensive absences from work. Malingerers frequently depict themselves and their prior functioning in exclusively complimentary terms (Layden 1966).

The malingerer may assert both the inability to work and the capacity for recreation. In contrast, the claimant with genuine PTSD is more likely to withdraw from recreational activities as well as work. The malingerer may pursue a legal claim tenaciously while alleging depression or incapacitation due to symptoms of PTSD (Davidson 1965).

Malingerers are unlikely to volunteer information about sexual dysfunction (Chaney et al. 1984; Sadoff 1978), although they generally are eager to emphasize their physical complaints. Malingerers are also unlikely to volunteer information about nightmares unless they have been coached or have read the diagnostic criteria for PTSD. When asked details about traumatic dreams, malingerers may give frequent replies of "I don't know."

Genuine nightmares experienced by civilians after trauma usually show variations on the theme of the traumatic event (Garfield 1987). For example, a woman who was raped may have dreams in which she feels helpless and is tortured without being raped. The malingerer who does not know the expected dream patterns may claim repetitive dreams that *always* reenact the traumatic event in exactly the same way. In posttraumatic nightmares of civilian adults, there is usually a fairly rapid fading of the nightmare in a few weeks. Posttraumatic nightmares, as contrasted with lifetime nightmares unrelated to trauma, are almost always accompanied by considerable body movement (van der Kolk et al. 1984).

Persons who have had true PTSD may exaggerate their symptoms or allege that symptoms persist when they no longer do. These are the most difficult cases to accurately assess because falsehood is never more persuasive than when it baits its hook with truth. Claimants who have had some genuine PTSD symptoms in the past have the advantage of knowing how to give accurate descriptions of PTSD symptoms.

Threshold Guidelines for a Full Assessment of Malingering

If the claimant shows one or more of the eight criteria listed in Table 6–2, the clinician should thoroughly investigate the possibility that a person is malingering PTSD. Special interview techniques, psychological testing, and, occasionally, inpatient evaluation should then be considered.

In my opinion, the clinician who suspects malingering may use certain interview stratagems because the use of subterfuge in assessing deceit is justified. Insurance companies routinely make surreptitious videotapes of suspected malingerers (Schafer 1986). When inquiring about the symptoms of PTSD, the clinician may ask about symptoms that are not typically seen in this disorder. For example, inquiry could be made about symptoms such as increased talkativeness, inflated self-esteem, or decreased need for sleep. Within earshot of the claimant, mention could also be made of a very atypical symptom, implying that it is usually present; the clinician can then see if the claimant complains of this symptom. In particularly difficult assessments, inpatient observation may be helpful in monitoring alleged symptoms, such as social withdrawal, sleep disturbance, or exaggerated startle reactions.

The Minnesota Multiphasic Personality Inventory (MMPI; Hathaway and McKinley 1989) is the most validated psychological test to ascertain malingered mental illness. Chaney et al. (1984) found that the MMPI can be helpful in distinguishing claimants with true PTSD from those with functional disorders. The MMPI profiles of persons with PTSD more closely resemble those of persons who have organic disease, with pain caused by organic pathology, than the profiles of persons with psychogenic pain and/or hypochondriasis. Clayer et al. (1984) developed an instrument, the Illness Behavior Questionnaire, that could distinguish among neurotic subjects, normal subjects, and individuals told to exaggerate their injury symptoms.

After completing a detailed examination and psychological testing, the clinician may decide to confront a claimant with his or her suspicions of malingering. Expressing a sympathetic understanding of the temptation to exaggerate symptoms of PTSD increases the likelihood that a claimant will

---

Table 6–2. Threshold model for the evaluation of malingering posttraumatic stress disorder

Any one of the following criteria:
- ❑ Poor work record
- ❑ Prior "incapacitating" injuries
- ❑ Discrepant capacity for work and recreation
- ❑ Unvarying, repetitive dreams
- ❑ Antisocial personality traits
- ❑ Overidealized functioning before the trauma
- ❑ Evasiveness
- ❑ Inconsistency in symptom presentation

acknowledge it; trying to shame the person is likely to increase anger and denial. The malingerer should be given every opportunity to save face. Once a person denies malingering, there is a risk that it will be harder to admit later. It is better to say, "You haven't told me the whole truth" than, "You have been lying to me" (Inbau and Reid 1967).

Guidelines for Assessment in Vietnam War Veterans

In 1979, the United States government initiated Operation Outreach to handle readjustment and psychiatric problems of Vietnam War veterans (Lynn and Belza 1984). Malingering PTSD became much easier after lists of PTSD symptoms were widely distributed by national service organizations (Atkinson et al. 1982). In addition, veterans with true PTSD at veterans centers and Veterans Administration (VA) hospitals provided other veterans with opportunities to become aware of PTSD symptoms (Lynn and Belza 1984).

Estimates of the prevalence of PTSD among Vietnam veterans have ranged from 20% to 70% (Ashlock et al. 1987; Friedman 1981; J. P. Wilson, unpublished observations, 1981). The incidence of malingered or factitious PTSD in the Reno, Nevada, VA Hospital was 7 of 125 patients hospitalized for PTSD in a 5-month period (Lynn and Belza 1984). This estimate (approximately 6%) may be conservative because only "severe" PTSD cases were hospitalized.

Vietnam veterans may be motivated to malinger PTSD for three primary reasons: 1) to obtain compensation, 2) to be admitted to a VA hospital, and 3) to reduce punishment for criminal conduct. Since the VA accepted the delayed type of PTSD as a potentially compensable disorder in 1980, obtaining compensation has been the primary motive for veterans to malinger PTSD (Bitzer 1990). When PTSD is malingered for the purpose of gaining hospital admission, it must be distinguished from factitious PTSD. In factitious disorders, a person intentionally produces symptoms because of a psychological need to assume a sick role, rather than external gains. Factitious PTSD allows a veteran to assume the patient role, whereas malingered PTSD serves other goals, such as providing refuge or documentary support for seeking compensation.

The following special guidelines for evaluating malingered PTSD in Vietnam veterans should be considered in addition to the general guidelines already suggested for civilians.

Special Guidelines for Collateral Data

Military records and eyewitness accounts are critical because they provide the only independent substantiation of the validity of the stressor. The veteran's spouse and/or relatives should be interviewed to validate current PTSD symptoms and assess premilitary behavioral adjustment.

It is often difficult to acquire third-party documentation of exposure to combat or other stresses during service in Vietnam. Personnel files are often not revealing. A veteran's unit history files (unit logs) and data from other members of the same unit are better resources. One simple procedure is to see whether the veteran's discharge papers (Form DD 214) indicate overseas service. Although discharge papers should also include campaign and service articles (Lynn and Belza 1984), the record of awards is not always complete (Early 1984). Because the veteran's discharge papers may be falsified, it is best to obtain a copy from the U.S. Department of Defense (Sparr and Atkinson 1986). VA medical centers have a national register that can supply information about prisoners of war with one phone call.

Graphic stories of battle are not conclusive proof of PTSD. The accounts presented by veterans malingering PTSD can be just as vivid and detailed as those presented by veterans with the genuine disorder (Hamilton 1985). Consultation with actual combat veterans can help pinpoint a veteran's lack of knowledge of the geography and culture of Vietnam (Lynn and Belza 1984). Ashlock et al. (1987) noted that some veterans with malingered PTSD were able to pass multiple screening interviews by both Vietnam veterans and staff. Several, however, were discovered by group members within the first 2 days of their program.

Special Guidelines for Information Obtained From the Claimant

The clinician should take a detailed military history and obtain details of military traumas; civilian stressors should also be reviewed.

To receive VA compensation, the severity of the stressor must be rated as "catastrophic" (Atkinson et al. 1982). The events most highly correlated with PTSD in Vietnam veterans are participation in atrocities and high numbers of combat stressors (Breslau and Davis 1987).

Special Guidelines for Clinician's Interview Style

Clinicians evaluating PTSD in Vietnam veterans must exercise extra care to maintain their objectivity.

Powerful emotions in clinicians may occur because of strong feelings for or against the Vietnam war. Recounting of gruesome events in Vietnam, expressions of painful affect, and outbursts of anger can be stressful for both claimants and clinicians (Atkinson et al. 1982). Some clinicians feel moved to diagnose PTSD on the basis of fragmentary symptoms because they feel a sense of moral responsibility for the Vietnam veteran as a victim (Atkinson et al. 1982; Pankratz 1985).

The antipathy many Vietnam veterans feel toward the federal government may interfere with the evaluation process (Atkinson et al. 1982). Some veterans find it very difficult to discuss their traumatic, painful memories—even with a sympathetic clinician. Authoritarian clinicians are especially unlikely to gain access to such data. Some veterans try to minimize their difficulty; other veterans exaggerate actual symptoms of PTSD for fear of failing to receive treatment or compensation (Fairbank et al. 1986).

Special Guidelines for Assessing the Differential Diagnosis of Malingered PTSD

The differential diagnosis of malingered Vietnam PTSD should include antisocial personality, factitious disorder, and genuine PTSD due to civilian stressors.

The differential diagnosis between antisocial personality and PTSD may be difficult. Although the presence of an antisocial personality disorder does not rule out PTSD, it should increase the clinician's index of suspicion regarding malingering. Unfortunately, many persons with PTSD have antisocial symptoms—such as an inconsistent work pattern, poor parenting, repeated legal difficulties, inability to maintain an enduring attachment with a sexual partner, episodes of irritability, reckless behavior, failure to honor financial obligations, and a history of impulsive behavior (Walker 1981). Veterans with PTSD may also show substance abuse, rage, and suspiciousness. Identification of developmental symptoms of antisocial personality disorder (i.e., before age 15) is critical. School records and family interviews are necessary to validate veterans' recollections.

New life stressors, such as divorce, unemployment, or legal problems, may occur after military discharge. The clinician must discern whether a claimant's PTSD is the result of the Vietnam experience or a nonmilitary stressor. A coexisting mental disorder, such as psychosis or depression, may further complicate the assessment (Atkinson et al. 1982).

Melton (1984) suggested several factors that help to differentiate the veteran with true PTSD from the malingerer. Whether the veteran attributes blame to self or others is one good discriminator. On the one hand, veterans with true PTSD are likely to feel intense levels of guilt and perceive themselves as the cause of their problems; they seem hesitant to blame their problems on the Vietnam War. On the other hand, malingerers are more likely to present themselves as victims of circumstance. They are likely to begin the session with statements that imply that their life predicaments are a direct result of their Vietnam experience; they condemn authority and the war. In the first visit, veterans with true PTSD are often resistant to openly admitting that their problems may be related to their experience in Vietnam. They are likely to come in because of family members' insistence or because of recurrent loss of employment, depression, outbursts of anger, or substance abuse (Melton 1984).

A common chief complaint in veterans with malingered PTSD is fear that they might lose control and harm others (Pankratz 1985); the expression of this fear is likely to gain them admission to psychiatric hospitals. Malingerers tend to overplay their Vietnam experience. They might say, "I've got PTSD. I've got flashbacks and nightmares. I'm really stressed out" (Merback 1984). Veterans with true PTSD are more likely to downplay their combat experience, such as by saying, "Lots of guys had it worse than me."

In veterans' posttraumatic nightmares, the encapsulated traumatic scene may become isolated; when activated, it runs off in an almost identical fashion for many years. After the fading of the initial posttraumatic nightmares, the veteran may begin to wake up terrified and report that he has dreamed of the horrible event exactly or almost exactly as it happened (van der Kolk et al. 1984). The themes of intrusive recollections and dreams are different in true and malingered PTSD. Veterans with PTSD often report themes of helplessness, guilt, or rage. Dreams in true PTSD generally convey a theme of helplessness with regard to the particular traumatic events that occurred during combat. In malingered PTSD, the themes of intrusive recollections are more often anger toward generalized authority; dreams emphasize themes of grandiosity and power (Melton 1984).

Differences have been observed between veterans with true and malingered PTSD in their expression and acknowledgment of feelings. In true PTSD, the veteran often denies or has numbed the emotional impact of combat. In malingered PTSD, the veteran will often make efforts to convince the clinician how emotionally traumatizing Vietnam was for him by "acting out" the alleged feelings. The true PTSD veteran generally *downplays* symptoms, whereas the malingerer *overplays* them. For instance, veterans with true PTSD try not to bring attention to their hyperalertness and suspicious eye movements. In contrast, PTSD malingerers present their suspiciousness with a dramatic quality, as if they were trying to draw attention to it. As a further example, PTSD malingerers may volunteer that they think of nothing but Vietnam and "relish" telling combat memories (Melton 1984).

An important characteristic of PTSD is the avoidance of environmental conditions associated with the trauma. For example, the PTSD veteran may stay home on hot rainy days because of the resemblance to Vietnam weather. Camping may be avoided because the veteran finds himself looking for trip wires in the bush. In addition, crowds may be avoided because combat usually occurred "in a crowd." In malingered PTSD, the veteran is unlikely to report having such postcombat reactions to environmental stimuli (Melton 1984).

Other characteristics have been noted that differentiate between actual and malingered PTSD in Vietnam veterans. These characteristics, shown in Table 6–3, include the ways in which guilt and anger are experienced. These clinical indicators for malingered Vietnam PTSD are based primarily on case reports and must therefore be considered tentative.

Special Guidelines for Threshold for Full Evaluation

If one or more indicators of malingered PTSD are evident (see Table 6–3), a more specialized assessment of malingering should be made. This should include detailed interviewing and psychological testing.

Fairbank et al. (1985) compared MMPI scores of Vietnam veterans with PTSD with those of a group of veterans instructed to malinger PTSD. The authors were able to accurately classify over 90% of the subjects. Similarly, Ashlock et al. (1987) noted differences in MMPI scores between veterans malingering PTSD and those who had genuine PTSD. Perconte and Goreczny (1990) did not confirm these findings. Dalton et al. (1986) found that PTSD appears to have a minimal effect on performance on neuropsychological tests.

In major evaluation centers, audiotapes of combat sounds should be considered as an assessment device to assess malingering. Blanchard et al. (1982) reported that they could discriminate with 95.5% accuracy between veterans suffering from genuine PTSD and a control group by playing an audiotape of combat sounds. They measured veterans' heart rates, systolic blood pressures, and muscle tension with a forehead electromyelogram. Measure of the heart rate alone allowed correct classification of 90.9%. More recent studies have also been encouraging (Orr et al. 1990; Pitman et al. 1987). However, Orr et al. (1993) found that 25% of non-PTSD subjects were able to simulate the physiologic responses of PTSD subjects.

Pitman et al. (1994) reported that one trial judge ruled against a challenge to the admission of psychophysiological assessment data to prove the PTSD criterion of "physiological reactivity on exposure to internal or external cues that symbolize or resemble an aspect of the traumatic event."

Table 6–3.   Clinical indicators of malingered Vietnam War posttraumatic stress disorder (PTSD)

Genuine PTSD	Malingered PTSD
Minimize relationship of symptoms to Vietnam	Emphasize relationship of symptoms to Vietnam
Blame themselves	Blame others
Dream themes of helplessness or guilt	Dream themes of grandiosity or power
Deny emotional impact of combat	"Act out" alleged feelings
Are reluctant to tell combat memories	"Relish" telling combat memories
Have survivor guilt related to specific incidents	Have generalized guilt over surviving the war
Avoid environments that resemble Vietnam	Do not avoid environments that resemble Vietnam
Show anger at helplessness	Show anger at authority

Such a procedure may be impractical for the individual clinician but could be quite helpful to professionals making frequent decisions about PTSD compensation. Psychophysiologic test results cannot be used alone to show the truth of PTSD. However, they may be very helpful along with other information in a forensic evaluation.

Special Guidelines for Veterans Facing Criminal Charges

In assessing the validity of the relationship between PTSD and a crime, the clinician should consider whether the crime scene re-creates the combat trauma, whether there was evidence of dissociation at the time of the criminal conduct, and whether there was a rational alternative motive for the crime.

In the criminal justice system, the diagnosis of PTSD may serve as a basis for an insanity defense, a reduction of charges, or a mitigation of penalty. Veterans who are charged with serious crimes may consequently be highly motivated to malinger PTSD or to falsely impute a causal link between a crime and genuine PTSD. Three clinical presentations have led to successful insanity defenses. First, a veteran may enter into a dissociative state due to a flashback and resort to survivor skills learned in Vietnam. Second, a veteran with severe survivor guilt may commit acts designed to result in his death in order to be reunited with buddies killed in action. Third, a veteran may engage in sensation-seeking behavior, such as drug trafficking, to relive combat excitement (J. P. Wilson, unpublished observations, 1981).

Conclusion

The assessment of malingered psychiatric symptoms after traumatic events is difficult because reports of subjective symptoms are difficult to verify. Clinicians must be thoroughly grounded in the phenomenology of PTSD and be aware of the common differences between those with genuine symptoms and their malingering counterparts. The guidelines that are proposed in this chapter emphasize the need for detailed history taking and independent corroboration to assess the possibility of malingering in PTSD claimants.

References

American Psychiatric Association: Diagnostic and Statistical Manual of Mental Disorders, 3rd Edition. Washington, DC, American Psychiatric Association, 1980

American Psychiatric Association: Diagnostic and Statistical Manual of Mental Disorders, 4th Edition. Washington, DC, American Psychiatric Association, 1994

Ashlock L, Walker J, Starkey TW, et al: Psychometric characteristics of factitious PTSD. VA Practitioner 4:37–41, 1987

Atkinson RM, Henderson RG, Sparr LF, et al: Assessment of Vietnam veterans for post-traumatic stress disorder in Veterans Administration disability claims. Am J Psychiatry 139:1118–1121, 1982

Bitzer R: Caught in the middle: mentally disabled veterans and the Veterans Administration, in Strangers at Home: Vietnam Veterans Since the War, 2nd Edition. Edited by Figley CR, Leventman S. New York, Brunner/Mazel, 1990, pp 305–323

Blanchard EB, Kolb LC, Pallmeyer TP, et al: A Psychophysiological study of post-traumatic stress disorder in Vietnam veterans. Psychiatr Q 54:220–229, 1982

Braverman M: Post-injury malingering is seldom a calculated ploy. Occup Health Saf 47:36–48, 1978

Breslau N, Davis GC: Post-traumatic stress disorder: the etiologic specificity of wartime stressors. Am J Psychiatry 144:578–583, 1987

Chaney HS, Cohn CK, Williams SG, et al: MMPI results: a comparison of trauma victims, psychogenic pain, and patients with organic disease. J Clin Psychol 40:1450–1454, 1984

Clayer JR, Bookless C, Ross MW: Neurosis and conscious symptom exaggeration: its differentiation by the illness behavior questionnaire. J Psychosom Res 28:237–241, 1984

Clevenger SV: Spinal Concussion. London, FA Davis, 1889

Dalton JE, Pederson SL, Blom BE, et al: Neuropsychological screening for Vietnam veterans with PTSD. VA Practitioner 3:37–47, 1986

Davidson HA: Malingered psychosis. Bull Menninger Clin 14:157–163, 1950

Davidson HA: Forensic Psychiatry, 2nd Edition. New York, Ronald Press, 1965

Early E: On confronting the Vietnam veteran (letter). Am J Psychiatry 141:472–473, 1984

Fairbank JA, McCaffrey RJ, Keane TM: Psychometric detection of fabricated symptoms of post-traumatic stress disorder. Am J Psychiatry 142:501–503, 1985

Fairbank JA, McCaffrey RJ, Keane TM: On simulating post-traumatic stress disorder (letter and reply). Am J Psychiatry 143:268–269, 1986

Friedman MJ: Post-Vietnam syndrome: recognition and management. Psychosomatics 22:931–943, 1981

Garfield P: Nightmares in the sexually abused female teenager. Psychiatric Journal of the University of Ottawa 12:93–97, 1987

Hamilton JD: Pseudo post-traumatic stress disorder. Mil Med 150:353–356, 1985

Hamilton JE: Railway and Other Accidents. London, Bailliere, Tindall & Co, 1906

Hathaway SR, McKinley JC: Minnesota Multiphasic Personality Inventory—2. Minneapolis, MN, University of Minnesota, 1989

Henderson J: Psychic trauma claims in civil and administrative law. Panel Presentation at the American Academy of Psychiatry and the Law Meeting, Philadelphia, PA, October 18, 1986

Hofling CK: Some psychologic aspects of malingering. General Practitioner 31:115–121, 1965

Hurst AF: Medical Diseases of War. London, Edward Arnold, 1940

Inbau FE, Reid JE: Criminal Interrogation and Confessions, 2nd Edition. Baltimore, MD, Williams & Wilkins, 1967

Jones AB, Llewellyn J: Malingering. London, Heinmann, 1917

Keiser L: The Traumatic Neurosis. Philadelphia, PA, JB Lippincott, 1968

Layden M: Symptoms separate hysteric, malingerer. Psychiatric Progress 1:7, 1966

Lipman FD: Malingering in personal injury cases. Temple Law Quarterly 35:141–162, 1962

Lishman WA: Organic Psychiatry. Oxford, UK, Blackwell Scientific Publication, 1978

Lynn EJ, Belza M: Factitious post-traumatic stress disorder: the veteran who never got to Vietnam. Hosp Community Psychiatry 35:697–701, 1984

Melton R: Differential diagnosis: a common sense guide to psychological assessment. Vet Center Voice Newsletter V:1–12, 1984

Merback K: The vet center dilemma: post-traumatic stress disorder and personality disorders. Vet Center Voice Newsletter V:6–7, 1984

Miller H, Cartlidge N: Simulation and malingering after injuries to the brain and spinal cord. Lancet 1:580–585, 1972

Orr SP, Claiborn JM, Altman B, et al: Psychometric profile of posttraumatic stress disorder, anxious, and healthy Vietnam veterans: correlations with physiologic responses. J Consult Clin Psychol 58:329–335, 1990

Ossipov VP: Malingering: the simulation of psychosis. Bull Menninger Clin 8:31–42, 1944

Pankratz L: The spectrum of factitious post-traumatic stress disorder. Paper presented at the annual meeting of the American Psychiatric Association, Dallas, TX, May 18–24, 1985

Perconte ST, Goreczny AJ: Failure to detect fabricated posttraumatic stress disorder with the use of the MMPI in a clinical population. Am J Psychiatry 147:1057–1060, 1990

Pitman RK, Orr SP, Forgue DF, et al: Psychophysiologic assessment of posttraumatic stress disorder imagery in Vietnam combat veterans. Arch Gen Psychiatry 44:970–975, 1987

RESTATEMENT OF TORTS § 588 (1938)

Sadoff RL: Personal Injury and the Psychiatrist (Lesson 38)—Weekly Psychiatry Update Series. Princeton, NJ, Biomedia, 1978

Schafer E: Workers Compensation Workshop. American Academy of Psychiatry and the Law Meeting, Philadelphia, PA, October 18, 1986

Sparr LF, Atkinson RM: Post-traumatic stress disorder as an insanity defense: medicolegal quicksand. Am J Psychiatry 143:608–613, 1986

Trimble MR: Post-Traumatic Neurosis From Railway Spine to the Whiplash. New York, Wiley, 1981 van der Kolk B, Blitz R, Burr W, et al: Nightmares and trauma: a comparison of nightmares after combat with lifelong nightmares in veterans. Am J Psychiatry 141:187–190, 1984

Walker JI: Vietnam combat veterans with legal difficulties: a psychiatric problem? Am J Psychiatry 138:1384–1385, 1981

Index

*Page numbers printed in **boldface** type refer to table or figures.*

A

Accident(s)
  of relative/friend, PTSD rate
    and, 49
  victims, PTSD rates of, 15
Action memory, 91
Acute stress disorder, DSM-IV
  diagnostic criteria, **40**
Adjustment disorder, 93
Adolescents, forensic psychiatric
  examination of, 85–96
  role of forensic clinician in,
    90–92
Aggravated assault, PTSD
  development, 15
Alcohol abuse, 14
Alcohol dependence, 14
Alphonso v. Charity Hospital, 4
AMA guides, 69
Amitriptyline, 19
Amnesia, secondary to head
  injury, 44
Anger, 34
Anhedonia, 41
Anterograde amnesia, 44
Antianxiety drugs, 61
Antidepressants, 61
Antipsychotics, 61
Antisocial behavior, 22
Antisocial personality disorder, 38,
  59
  comorbidity with PTSD, 16
  differential diagnosis, 27

Anxiety
  PTSD risk and, 22
  substance abuse and, 102
Anxiety disorders
  after trauma, 122
  PTSD classification and, 45–46
  PTSD development and, 73, 89
  PTSD differential diagnosis
    and, 93
Assault, 3
Assessment, forensic
  of functional impairment, 66–76
  impact of psychiatric history on,
    61–62
  multiple data sources, 100–101
  psychiatric examination for. *See*
    Psychiatric examination,
    forensic
  standard, of functional
    psychiatric impairment,
    75–76
  of traumatized children, 93–95
Attorneys, presence during
  forensic evaluation, 71–72
Automobile accidents, 4
Avoidance
  in children, 91–92
  of family responsibilities, 41
  symptoms, 41
Axis I disorders
  coexistence with PTSD, 61
  diagnosis of PTSD and, 36
  preexisting, 58–59

Axis I disorders *(continued)*
  PTSD and, 102
  trauma exposure and, 25
  traumatic stressors and, 51, 54
Axis II disorders
  coexistence with PTSD, 61
  diagnosis of PTSD and, 36
  preexisting, 58–59
  psychological testing for, 67
  traumatic stressors and, 51, 54
Axis III disorders, coexistence with
    PTSD, 61
Axis IV disorders, 68, 102
Axis V disorders, 68–69, 102

B

Barefoot v. Estelle, 4
Battery, 3
Battle fatigue, 32. See also
    Posttraumatic stress disorder
    (PTSD)
Behavior therapy, for intrusive
    symptoms, 75
Bereavement, 15, 48
Biologic studies, 26
Blood pressure, 130
Borderline personality disorder
    (BPD), 25, 38, 59
Brief Psychiatric Rating Scale
    (BPRS), 67
Brief reactive psychosis, 38
Buffalo Creek flood disaster, 70, 74
Business reverses, 48

C

California Workers' Compensation
    rating system, 44
CAPS (Clinician-Administered
    PTSD Scale), 105

Carter v. Gen. Motors, 4
Child/children
  dissociative identity disorder, 59
  forensic psychiatric
      examination of, 85–96
  illegal activities of, 21
  molestation, PTSD
      development and, 15
  neglect of, 87
  physical abuse of, 14, 60, 87
    combat-related PTSD and, 51
    dissociative identity disorder
        and, 59
  psychiatric evaluation of
    common pitfalls in, 95
    guidelines for, 95–96
    psychiatric outcome and,
        87–89
    role of forensic clinician in,
        90–92
    in trauma, 93–95
  with PTSD
    longitudinal study of, 17–18
    prognosis for, 92–93
    symptoms of, 89
  rape, by family member, 56
  repetitive play and, 91
  sexual abuse of, 14, 59–60, 87
  as trauma/violence witnesses,
      86, 87
  of Vietnam War veterans with
      PTSD, 93
Chowchilla school bus
    kidnapping, 59–60, 89
Civil trials, 5
Claimants
  Axis IV psychosocial and
      environmental problems
      and, 57–58
  future treatment, 74–75

information from, 121, 126
interview style guidelines for, 121
involvement in litigation as stressor, 74
malingering in. *See* Malingering
prognosis, 74–75, **75**
Clinical interview, 99, 100
Clinical interviews, of children, 94
Clinician, forensic. *See* Examiners, forensic
Clinician-Administered PTSD Scale (CAPS), 105
Cocaine-opiate users, 61
Coexisting disorders. *See* Comorbidity
Cognitive impairments, 42
Collateral data
evaluation of malingering and, 120–121
guidelines for, 120
for Vietnam War veterans, 126
Combat stress reactions (CSRs), 4, 18, 21
Community, psychiatric outcome of traumatized children and, 88–89
Comorbidity, 102
Axis I, 58–59
Axis II, 58–59
development/maintenance of PTSD symptoms and, 52, 54, 60
with multiple psychological stressors, 57
of psychiatric disorders, 15–17, **60**
Competence, to evaluate PTSD, 7
Complex posttraumatic stress disorder, 59

Comprehensive evaluation, 100
Concentration camp necrosis, 32. See also Posttraumatic stress disorder (PTSD)
Concentration difficulties, 34, 42
Conceptual models, 100
Constriction, 41
Construct validity studies, 45
Contagion, 93
Conversion disorders, 38, 122
Courts, use of DSM criteria, 44–45
Credibility, of treating psychiatrist, 64
Criminal charges, Vietnam War veterans facing, guidelines for, 131
Criterion A, 48
Cryptotrauma, 54
CSRs (combat stress reactions), 18

D
Data collection, multiple methods, 100–101
Daubert v. Merrel Dow Pharmaceuticals, 9
Death of loved one, 21
Defensive Styles Rating Scale, 68
Delayed onset posttraumatic stress disorder, 34, 36, 41, 55, 66
Denial, 41, 90
Depersonalization disorder, 38
Depersonalization event, 42
Depression
after trauma, 122
in children, 89
comorbidity with PTSD, 16
posttraumatic, 44
precrime, 22
with PTSD, 16, 102

Depression *(continued)*
  PTSD differential diagnosis
      and, 93
  risk, in PTSD, 73
  substance abuse and, 102
  symptoms, 34
  trauma exposure and, 101
  traumatic exposure and, 14, 22,
      25
Desensitization, 19
DESNOS (disorder of extreme
    stress not otherwise specified),
    24
Developmental skills, loss of, 92
Diagnosis, PTSD, 32, 99
  criteria, 34–47
    DSM-IV, **37–38, 39**
      vs. postconcussion syndrome
          criteria, **43**
    definition of traumatic event
        and, 48
    ignoring basic criteria in, 46–47
    multiple measures for, 106
    nomenclature
      in DSM-III, 3–4
      expansion, 4
      future of PTSD litigation and,
          5–6
      historical background, 1–3
      in individual cases, 6
    physiological component, 108
Diagnostic Interview Scale
    (DIS-NIMH), 104
Disaster(s)
  man-made, 4
  mass, 31
  natural, 4
    longitudinal studies, 19
  technological, longitudinal
      studies, 19

victims, 15, 16
Discriminant validity studies, 45
DIS-NIMH (Diagnostic Interview
    Scale), 104
Disorder of extreme stress not
    otherwise specified
    (DESNOS), 24
Dissociative amnesia, 38
Dissociative fugue, 38
Dissociative identity disorder, 14,
    25, 38, 59
Dissociative phenomena, 59
Divorce, 128
Dohmann v. Richard, 72
Double depression, 102
Dream anxiety disorder, 38
Dreams, traumatic, 42, 91, 121
Drug abuse, 14, 31
Drug dependence, 14
Drug treatment. *See* Medications
DSM, PTSD diagnosis in, 13, 32, 46
DSM-II, PTSD diagnosis in, 32
DSM-III
  avoidance criteria of, 92
  nomenclature for PTSD, 3–4
  PTSD diagnostic criteria, 32, 45
    interrater and test-retest
        reliability, 45
DSM-III-R
  avoidance criteria of, 92
  Axis IV, 50
  Axis V, 68–69
  chronic PTSD diagnosis and, 36
  multiaxial evaluation system, 68
  PTSD diagnostic criteria, 4, 34,
      35–36, 39, 44
    misuse in litigation, 46
    prototypical case, 45
  PTSD symptoms and, 85
  PTSD variants and, 44

Severity of Psychological
Stressors Scale, 51
stressor definition, 23, 48
symptom development and, 48
trauma-related disorders, 38
DSM-IV
acute stress disorder diagnosis,
36
avoidance criteria, 92
Axis V, 68–69
chronic PTSD diagnosis and, 36
criterion A type, 15
draft criteria for PTSD, 23
field trials and, 23–25, 49
multiaxial evaluation system, 68
normative criterion, 50
personality disorders, 59
PTSD definition, 26
PTSD diagnostic criteria, 4, 32,
34, **37–38,** 39, 77, 117
clinically significant distress
and, 66
prototypical case and, 44–45
for acute stress disorder, **40**
changes in, **39**
for children and
adolescents, 85–86
misuse in litigation, 46
prototypical case, 45
PTSD symptoms and, 4
stressor criteria for PTSD, 48
DSM-V, Axis IV, 50
Dysthymia, with major depression,
102

E

Eating disorders, 25
Eggshell skull or psyche plaintiff,
53

Emotional constriction, 41
Environmental conditions,
avoidance in PTSD, 129
Epidemiologic Catchment Area
Studies, 21
Estrangement, 41
Evidence, rules of, 2
Examiners, forensic, 7, 36, 38
AMA guides and, 69
assessment methods for, 69
capacity to consent, 7
in evaluation of
children/adolescents,
90–92
interview style, for Vietnam War
veterans, 127
proposed guideline for, 47
psychological testing and, 67
standard questions for, 32–33
subjective reporting of PTSD
and, 62–66
Expert witnesses
admissibility of testimony, 2
qualification, 6–7
testimony, 4
treating psychiatrist as, 64–65
Explosive violent outbursts, 41

F

Facial muscle tension, 63
Fact witness, 65
Factitious disorder, 119
False imprisonment, 3
False imputation, 119
Family disruption, 73
Family members
interviews of, 120–121
presence during forensic
evaluation, 72

Fear, 48, 72
Federal Rules of Evidence, 4
Females, PTSD risk and, 22, 26
Field trials, 23–25
  DSM-IV, 49
  NIMH-sponsored, 45
Flashbacks, 34, 41, 42
  of childhood abuse, 60
  litigation involvement and, 74
  recurring, 44
Forensic psychiatric experts, 65
  subjective reporting of PTSD
       symptoms and, 65–66
  vs. treating psychiatrist,
       63–64
Forseeability, 5, 9
Fraud, 3
Freud, Anna, 86
Freud, Sigmund, 86
Functional impairment,
  assessment, 66–76

G
GAD. *See* Generalized anxiety
  disorder (GAD)
GAF (Global Assessment of
  Functioning Scale), 68
*Gammons v. Osteopathic Hospital of
  Maine, Inc.,* 53
GARF (Global Assessment of
  Relational Functioning), 68
GAS (Global Assessment Scale),
  67
General adaptation syndrome,
  stages, 41
Generalized anxiety disorder
  (GAD)
  with PTSD, 16
  trauma exposure and, 101

Georgetown University practice
  standards, for forensic
  evaluation, 6
Global Assessment of Functioning
  Scale (GAF), 68
Global Assessment of Relational
  Functioning (GARF), 68
Global Assessment Scale (GAS), 67
Grief, 89, 93
*Guidelines for Handling Psychiatric
  Issues in Workers' Compensation,*
  69
*Guides to Evaluation of Permanent
  Impairment,* 69
Guilt, 128

H
Hallucinations, 42
Hearsay, 8
Heart rates, 63, 130
Helplessness, 48
Hindsight bias, 5
Hostility, 34
Hyperactivity, 41
Hyperarousal, 41
Hyperarousal-intrusive symptoms,
  41
Hypnosis, 19

I
ICD-10, 24
IES (Impact of Event Scale), 19
Illness
  chronic, 48
  coexisting. *See* Comorbidity
  life-threatening, PTSD
       development and, 87
Imipramine, for intrusion
  symptoms, 19

Impact of Event Scale (IES), 19, 103, 107
Individual susceptibility, 54
Industrial accidents, 4
Insanity defense, 32
Interpersonal disruption, 73
Interviews. *See* Clinical interviews
Intrafamilial violence, 87
Intrusive symptoms, 41
    in children, 91
    types, 42
Invasive medical procedures, 78
Invisible trauma, 54

J

Johnson v. May, 4
Judicial determinations, 7–8

K

Keane PTSD Scale of the MMPI, 103, 106

L

Lay witness testimony, 2
Legal problems, of Vietnam War veterans, 128
Liability, 5
Licensure, expert witness qualification and, 7
Life stressors, 128
Life threats
    children and, 89
    illness, 26
    PTSD development, 15
    trauma, 53
Litigant. *See* Claimants
Litigation, 31
    admission of PTSD testimony, 56
    credibility issues in, 64

defendants, not guilty by reason of insanity, 32
effect on PTSD symptomatology/ impairment, 74
eggshell skull or psyche plaintiff, 53
future of, 5, 9
laboratory testing and, 63
misuse of PTSD diagnosis in, 46, 49
Longitudinal assessment, 17–20, 71
Lynch v. Knight, 2

M

Malingering, 3, 8, 62, 66
    assessment
        audiotapes of combat sounds for, 130
        guidelines for Vietnam War veterans, 125–131, **130**
        subterfuge in, 123–124
        threshold guidelines for, 123
    characteristics of malingerers, 122–123
    confirmation of diagnosis, 119–120
    defined, 118–119
    differential diagnosis, 122
    evaluation guidelines, 120–125
    incidence of, 119
    motivation for, 117–118, 125
    partial, 119
    pure, 119
    reluctance to diagnose, 119–120
    suspicion of, 117
    threshold model for evaluation, **124**
Marital affair, 54

Marital discord, 48
Marital disruption, 21
Medications
    assessment of functional
        impairments and, 71
    for intrusive symptoms, 75
    for pain, 61
    for psychiatric and physical
        disorders, 60
Memory
    action, 91
    disturbances, assessment in
        child, 92
    nonintrusive *vs.* reflection of
        traumatic event, 73
    short-term deficits, 42, 44
Men, PTSD rate and, 49
Mind-body duality, 3
Minnesota Multiphasic Personality
    Inventory (MMPI), 100, 124
    scores of Vietnam veterans,
        130130
Miscarriage, 54
Mississippi PTSD Scale, 100, 103,
    106–107
Mixed personality disorders, 59
MMPI (Minnesota Multiphasic
    Personality Inventory), 124
MMPI-2 (Minnesota Multiphasic
    Personality Inventory-2), 106
Mood changes, chronic, 59
Motivation
    for malingering, 117–118, 125
    for recovery, 72
Motor vehicle accident victims, 49
    head injury and, 122
    PTSD rates of, 15
Multiple personality disorder. *See*
    Dissociative identity disorder
Muscle tension, 130

N

National Institute of Mental
    Health (NIMH), 45
National Vietnam Veterans
    Readjustment Study (NVVRS),
    106
National Vietnam War veteran
    study, 17
Natural disaster victims, 19, 48
    functional psychiatric
        impairment over time, 73
Negligence, 3
Neuroses, traumatic, 22, 85, 118
Nightmares, 41, 42
    of childhood abuse, 60
    litigation involvement and, 74
    malingerers and, 123
    recurring, 44
    of Vietnam War veterans, 128
NIMH (National Institute of
    Mental Health), 45
*Nixon v. Mr. Property Management
    Co.*, 5
Nonphysical harm, recovery for, 3
Numbing, emotional, 34, 41
    in children, 91–92
    of PTSD, substance abuse and,
        102
NVVRS (National Vietnam
    Veterans Readjustment Study),
    106

O

Obsessive-compulsive disorder,
    with PTSD, 16
Occupational impairment, 73
Outcome, psychiatric
    stressor intensity and, 20
    in traumatized children, 87–89

P

Pain medications, 61
Palsgraf v. Long Island R.R., 5
Panic, 25, 101
Parental loss, 86
Parental separation, early, 22
Peer relations, psychiatric
    outcome of traumatized
    children and, 89
Penn Inventory for PTSD, 107–108
Personality changes, 59, 73
Personality disorders, 25
    preexisting, 58–59
    psychological testing for, 67
Personality questionnaires, 100
Phenelzine, for intrusion
    symptoms, 19
Phobic disorders, 14, 16, 25
Physical abuse, childhood, 59, 60
Physical assault victims
    PTSD development, 15
    PTSD rate and, 15, 49
Physical conditions, chronic,
    posttraumatic stress disorder
    and, 31
Physical damage claims, 3
Plaintiff, supersensitive, 53
Play, repetitive, 91
Poisoning, 54
Postconcussion syndrome
    after trauma, 122
    diagnostic criteria, *vs.*
        posttraumatic stress
        disorder criteria, **43**
    symptoms, 42, 122
Posttraumatic stress disorder
    (PTSD)
    acute onset, 69–70
    assessment, advances, 100

chronic, 70, 73
    combat-related, childhood
        physical abuse and, 51
    comorbidity. *See* Comorbidity
    complex, 59
    delayed onset, 34, 36
    development, after trauma
        exposure, risk factors for, 52
    diagnosis. *See* Diagnosis, PTSD
    epidemiology, in children, 86–87
    evaluation
        forensic relationship
            establishment, 7
        information used in, 8
        methods, 7–8
        presentation of results, 8
        videotaping, 8
    factitious. *See* Malingering
    genetic susceptibility, 51
    incidence, 31
    individual differences in, 20–23
    intrusion symptoms,
        pharmacologic treatment
        of, 19
    longitudinal studies, 17–20
    misdiagnosis, 41
    names for, **118**
    natural, uncomplicated course
        of, 69
    prognosis, in children, 92–93
    rates, 14–15, 25
    risk factors, 21–23, 26
    stages, 69
    stressor criterion, in DSM-III-R
        and DSM-IV, 45
    subjective reporting, 62–66
    susceptibility, 41, 51
    symptoms. *See* Symptoms, PTSD
    treatment, 72–73
        length of, 75

POWs (prisoners of war), 49, 73–74
Preexisting disorders
    medical, 60
    psychological, 102
Pretrauma functioning, of
    traumatized child, 94
Privilege, 8
Proximate cause, 5
Pseudo-PTSD, 55
Psychiatric disorders
    coexistence with PTSD, 61
    posttraumatic stress disorder
        and, 31
    prior history of, 53–54
Psychiatric examination, forensic,
    113. *See also* Psychological
    assessment, forensic
    attorney presence during, 71–72
    of children/adolescents, 85–96
        epidemiology, 86–87
        history, 86
    developmental focus, 90–91
    diagnostic criteria for PTSD,
        34–47
    evaluating traumatic stressor,
        48–58
    family member presence
        during, 72
    functional impairment
        assessment, 66–76
    guidelines, **33**
    of PTSD claimants, 31–77
    report
        collateral reports and, 112
        diagnostic formulation in,
            112–113
        examination and special test
            results, 111–112
        forensic case formulation, 112
        limits of confidentiality of, 110

    methods of assessment, 111
    multiaxial classification and,
        112–113
    referral questions for, 110
    referral source for, 110
    review of records, 111
    template for, **110**
    scheduling, 67
    standard questions for, 32–33
    of traumatized children
        common pitfalls in, 95
        guidelines for, 95–96
Psychiatric history
    impact on assessment, 61–62
    preexisting, 58–62
Psychiatrist, treating
    conflict of interest, 64
    credibility of, 64
    double-agent roles, 65
    as expert witness, 64–65
    impartial evaluations by, 7
    practice standards, 7
    subjective reporting of PTSD
        symptoms and, 65–66
    vs. forensic psychiatric expert,
        63–64
Psychodynamic treatment, 19
Psychological assessment, forensic,
    99, 103–109. *See also*
    Psychiatric examination,
    forensic
    consequences of trauma
        exposure and, 101
    preexisting psychological
        disorders and, 102
    psychometric measures, 105–108
    of PTSD, 101–103
    PTSD as secondary event and,
        101–102
Psychological challenge, 108

Psychological testing, as adjunct to forensic exam, 67
Psychometric measures, 105–108
  advantages of, 105
Psychophysiologic reactivity criteria, for PTSD, 63
Psychophysiologic studies, 62–63, 108–109
Psychoses, after trauma, 122
Psychotropic drugs, for PTSD, 72
PTSD. *See* Posttraumatic stress disorder (PTSD)
PTSD Interview, 104

R
Rage, 128
Railway spine, 2, 32
Rape, 14. *See also* Stressors
  PTSD development, 15
  trauma syndrome, 6, 56
  victims
    PTSD rate and, 15, 49
    spontaneous recovery of, 70
    stress inoculation for, 19
Recovery, motivation for, 72
Reenactment behavior, 91
Reexperiencing phenomenon, 42
Reliability, 45
REM sleep, recurrent posttraumatic nightmares and, 44
Retrograde amnesia, 44
Rules of evidence, 8

S
SAD (Standard Assessment of Depressive Disorders), 67
Salley v. Childs, 53
SCID, 103

Secondary traumatization, 93
Selective psychogenic amnesia, 42
Self abuse, 59
Self-destructive acts, 73
Self-report instruments, 67
Sensitive person, *vs.* supersensitive plaintiff, 53
Sexual abuse, childhood, 59, 60
Sexual assault victims
  PTSD rate and, 13, 14, 15, 49
  stressor criterion and, 23
Sexual dysfunction, with PTSD, 16
Sexual molestation, 15
Shell shock, 2, 32
SI-PTSD (Structured Interview for PTSD), 104–105
Sleep disturbances, 88
Sleep medications, 61
Sleeplessness, 34
Social Adjustment Scale, 100
Social and Occupational Functioning Assessment Scale (SOFA), 68
Social isolation, 41
Social role functioning, assessment, 101
SOFA (Social and Occupational Functioning Assessment Scale), 68
Somatization disorders, 25, 38
Spencer v. General Electric Company, 56
Spousal abuse, 14
Standard Assessment of Depressive Disorders (SADD), 67
Startle response, 41
State v. Kim, 56
Sterling v. Velsicol Chemical Corp, 55–56

Stressful life events, schematic
    chronology of, 69–71
Stressor(s), 4, 31–32, 34
    criteria, 23
    defined, 51
    degree of exposure, PTSD
        development and, 87
    dose or intensity of, 48
    DSM-III-R definition, 48
    evaluating, 48–58
    intensity or severity, 26
        duration and, 52
        individual differences in,
            20–21
        outcome and, 20
    involvement in litigation, 74
    low-magnitude, 54
    man-made *vs.* natural, 49
    normative gatekeeper
        definition of, 54
    preceding living patterns and,
        121
    PTSD qualifying, PTSD
        development and, 50
    subjective dimension, 48
    sufficiency of, 56–57
    threshold effect and,
        20–21
    type, 21
Stressor-susceptibility model of
    PTSD, 51
Structured Clinical Interview for
    DSM-III-R (SCID), 100
Structured Interview for PTSD
    (SI-PTSD), 104–105
Structured interviews, 103–105
Substance abuse, 25, 73, 128
    with PTSD, 16, 102
    trauma exposure and, 101
Subthreshold PTSD, 50

Sudden death of relative/friend,
    PTSD rate and, 49
Suicide, posttraumatic stress
    disorder and, 31
Support, psychological,
    perceptions, PTSD
    development and, 52
Suspiciousness, 128
Sweat gland activity, 63
Symptom Checklist-90 (SCL-90),
    PTSD scale, 107
Symptoms, PTSD, 4
    absence of, 41
    in adults *vs.* children, 89
    antisocial, 127–128
    in children, 88, 89
    commingling with traumatic
        memories, 60
    criteria, 34
    development, 48
    downplaying of, 129
    historical aspects of, 85
    insufficient to meet DSM-III-R
        and DSM-IV PTSD
        criteria, 39
    intrusive, 20
    misinterpretation of, 41–42
    as normal response to trauma,
        54
    numbing, 20
    overplaying of, 129
    proximate cause of, 58
    psychological, functional
        impairment and, 67–68
    reexperiencing, 42
    spontaneous recovery, 69–70
    subjective, 117
    subjective reporting of, 62–66
    worsening, in absence of
        treatment, 70–71

T

Technological disasters,
  longitudinal studies, 19
Terror, 48
Theriaulta v. Swan, 53
Threat to life, PTSD rate and, 49
Tort law, 2–3, 9
  litigation, 4, 54–55, 55
  rules, 5
Torture, 49. *See also* Stressors
Toxic substance exposure,
  54–55
Trauma exposure
  definition, objective criteria for,
    25
  disorders associated with, 101
  epidemiology, in general
    population, 13–14
  multiple, 26
  PTSD development after, risk
    factors for, 22, 52
  PTSD rates after, 14–15
  related disorders, in DSM-III-R,
    38
  risk factors for, 52
Traumatic necrosis, 32. See also
  Posttraumatic stress disorder
  (PTSD)
Traumatic stressor. *See* Stressor
Traumatization, hindsight, 55
Treatment information, release of,
  64
Triggering event. *See* Stressor
Trust, 53
Twin studies, 20

U

Unemployment, 128

V

V code, 54
Victim rights, 32
Victimization
  crime, 13
  PTSD rate and, 49
  sexual, 13–14
*Victorian Railway Commissioners v.
  Coultas,* 3
Vietnam War veterans, 15, 86
  collateral data guidelines, 126
  comorbid conditions of,
    15–16
  facing criminal charges, 131
  genuine *vs.* malingered PTSD,
    clinical indicators of, **130**
  information from, 126
  malingering assessment,
    guidelines for, 125–131,
    130
  with PTSD, children of, 93
  PTSD prevalence in, 125
  PTSD rate and, 49
  PTSD symptoms and, 70–71
  stressor severity, 20
  threshold for full evaluation,
    guidelines for, 129
  true *vs.* malingered PTSD,
    128–129

W

Withdrawal, 41
Witnessing of trauma, children
  and, 89
Women, PTSD rate and, 49

Z

Zebo v. Houston, 69